T0367948

A GOOD SIGNATURE

A GOOD SIGNATURE

STELLA EBURUO

ARCHWAY
PUBLISHING

Archway Publishing books may be ordered through booksellers or by contacting:

Archway Publishing
1663 Liberty Drive
Bloomington, IN 47403
www.archwaypublishing.com
844-669-3957

ISBN: 978-1-6657-6556-5 (sc)
ISBN: 978-1-6657-6558-9 (hc)
ISBN: 978-1-6657-6557-2 (e)

Library of Congress Control Number: 2024919750

Print information available on the last page.

Archway Publishing rev. date: 09/12/2024

Donald J. Trump, the forty-fifth president of the United States of America, was born in New York, New York, to the handsome Fred Trump and the beautiful Mary Anne Trump. Fred Trump was a successful high-end real estate mogul, and his little boy Donald watched his father closely and attentively. As if he could predict what the future held in store for his son, Fred trained Donald very well as the boy was eager to know everything. Donald John Trump had many choices and talents in life—he went to military school, was a businessman, and was a TV star—but he chose the same occupation as his father, namely, real estate. Donald promised his father that he was going to turn one million dollars into billions of dollars and that he would change the skyline of New York City. His father listened and believed him, and the rest is history. Donald Trump did indeed change the skyline of New York City, and he is a billionaire. He loves his country, the United States. Trump is abundantly blessed in real estate and everything he puts his hand to. He is a happy man, blessed with five exceptional children: Ivanka, Donald Jr., Eric, Tiffany, and Barron. He is married to a model, the beautiful Melania Trump, who gave birth to Barron. A wealthy man, Trump owns the Mar-a-Lago Club, has houses around the United States and in other countries, and has companies, hotels, airplanes, casinos, golf clubs, and other businesses, a philantropist. He likes gold, and some of the fixtures in his houses and airplanes are decorated with real gold. He has been blessed and has been successful in the United States and around the world. No wonder people say that everything he touches turns to gold.

Trump, wanting to pay back his country, decided to run for president to make the United States great again. He wanted to fix the country and keep it from crumbling and going in the wrong direction. The infrastructure, the economy, national security, health care, education, jobs, borders, free speech, and lawlessness were a few areas he targeted for improvement. He wanted to take care of the citizens, especially the middle class, which has been forgotten for a long time, and veterans. Trump campaigned hard with his exceptional children and beautiful wife Melania, who is tall, tough, thoughtful, and family-oriented. On one of her campaign stops, she told the audience that her husband was not a career politician, that he wanted to serve the land that has favored him and blessed him so much. On another stop during the campaign, she told the crowd that her husband was a good man. "He gets things done," she said. "He is fair and treats everyone equally, but if he is punched or attacked, he will punch back ten times harder."

It was a big battle between Donald Trump and the sixteen other candidates, all experienced career politicians, but Trump ended up winning the 2016 presidential election. On January 20,

2017, he was sworn in and became the forty-fifth president of the United States of America.

A good signature is equal to a good president because such a president only signs legislation that matters, things that will be positive for the country, not work against the country. Some people think a president should always be a lawyer, but I think a good president can be of any vocation—lawyer, doctor, movie star, real estate agent, farmer, carpenter, teacher, and so forth. Some politicians think a good president will always come from their own party, but I do not see it that way. I believe a good president can come from either of the parties. A good president who has a good signature can be a Democrat, a Republican, or an Independent. Why do you think our founding fathers set things up like that, Democrat, Republican, and Independent? So that nobody would be left out and so that people would be able to make their own choices of whom they want to vote for, not having to vote for candidates whom others want them to vote for.

Because of politics and politicians, sometimes we miss out on electing a well-mannered individual who would make a good president for the whole country and even positively influence the world. Donald Trump and Ronald Reagan were not politicians, but they did remarkably well accomplishing their jobs. A good president can be a man or woman, can be young or old, and can be an Independent, a Republican, or a Democrat. A good president is able to sign into law legislation that protects freedom of speech and also freedom of religion. A good president can be of any religion or denomination. I belong to a Christian denomination, but sometimes I preach that doing good is my religion. Anyone running for president of the United States should have the characteristics necessary for governing and serving the people of the United States of America, including dealmaking, because as commander in chief, one needs to show up in force.

Sometimes a president makes a brilliant deal for the country or with entities outside it. The

United States is the greatest country in the whole wide world, and it should have good leadership, good governance, and freedom. The president we Americans choose should be able to win over our adversaries for peacekeeping in the world and also maintain ties with all our allies, such as Israel, our biggest ally of all time.

The foregoing are the reasons why people from other countries bet their lives to come to live in the United States, the land of the brave and the home of the free. Human beings still lose their lives trying to cross the border into this country. People sail the seven seas trying to arrive at this land of freedom. Their boats might accidentally capsize, and many may end up being swallowed by the big ocean, losing their lives. Some may end up being swallowed by the white sand of the desert because the walk is very hot and very long. Some will cut unimaginable deals trying to reach this land, and some will sell everything they own and jump into airplanes to be transported to the other side of the world to enter the United States of America—a bold act, committed for the purposes of making a better life and having a fulfilling future in this country. Others will take their children on this journey, maybe through a jungle or a forest, and in any weather, without anything—no food, no drink, and no money in their pockets, not knowing if they will make it.

Why do you think such people risk their lives to come to the United States? It is because of freedom, the possibility of greener pastures, and a love for humanity. Given the greatness the United States possesses, it is worth it to give it a try. Now it is obvious that border walls work. If the door is closed, then the migrants will go back. Then they can only imagine the greatness of this country—a land where no matter if you are rich or poor, you will enjoy the flowing milk and honey and the grace of God.

Please permit me to express my condolences to all who suffered death while looking forward to greener pastures abroad, running away from war, torture, hunger, death, and abuse. I am sorry for what happened to you. I shed tears for you all. I send condolence cards and flowers. May your gentle souls rest in peace, especially those of you who are African descendants.

A president of the United States should be somebody who is always ready to work tirelessly for the American people, which is one of the characteristics of former president Trump in his four years in the White House. He also had a vision for space, including the Moon and Mars. A president of this country will be strong in body, spirit, and mind. Being on the debate stage with a fan blowing between your legs is not the perfect look or a strong look for a presidential candidate. That is one of the reasons debates are essential every election year—so that voters are able to see and pick a candidate who will make a good commander in chief. Sometimes nation will rise against nation and kingdom against kingdom. A US president shall rule with power through strength. A presidential candidate who cannot deliver on the debate stage also cannot deliver on the world stage. Our president should be fearless, one of the greatest dealmakers of all time, a person with a good signature, a peacemaker, and someone who can work tirelessly for this country. A US president should be able to give a good handshake. He or she should be a God-fearing person who understands that to lead means to serve, and he or she should be ready to serve with all his or her heart, using the best leadership style, which every Christian leader should possess. A good leader invokes the servant style of leadership and stands tall on the world stage. Such a person will make a good president of the United States.

A US president should always remember that this country will always be the greatest country on earth and should do everything possible to keep it great and on top at all times. May the United States of America forever continue to be the greatest country on earth. Amen.

A person vying for the US presidency must have good abilities, including peacemaking and flexibility, which can help in dealmaking. The person should be very smart, as a smart leader will rule for a long time in a land where people obey the law. The world nowadays is changing on all fronts. We see good and bad, and we see wars, but with a president who is smart, is wise, and loves peace, countries who are our enemies can possibly turn back to being our friends or at least be able to work with us and strive for a deeper friendship so that we can become business partners and do business together again. Peace in different parts of the world is possible, for instance, in South Sudan, North Korea, South Korea, and the Middle East (including Israel and Palestine), to name but a few. A US president with a good signature should also be able to unify the two parties, Democrat and Republican, so that we may be one nation under God and indivisible. A US president should not be shy but outspoken, should always stand on his or her own two feet to command, and should address issues concerning the nation because he or she is its commander in chief. A president who is outspoken may be able to protect and defend US citizens, call for the release and return home of US citizens who are detained for political and nonpolitical reasons, and make deals to see the return of our country's forgotten treasures left abroad by previous administrations. Assuming the predecessor or previous administration made a trade deal or signed a treaty that is no longer doing our country any good or a treaty that has been abused or broken by the other president or other country, maybe by exceeding a range that was agreed upon, for example, for ammunition or manufacturing war equipment, chemicals, bombs, or rockets siloed underground, a good president with a good signature will be able to handle these things and do something about the situation. Perhaps he or she will impose a heavy fine, withdraw from the treaty, ban the offending country from a certain association or organization, strike the particular site, or peacefully sanction the offending country. Most importantly, a good president will opt out from any bad treaty and will always make sure the deal is right before he or she puts his or her signature on the treaty or borrows money from another country, which should not happen in the first place. Even excess use of the military by other countries should be properly dealt with.

A good president carefully watches over US military troops who are here in-country or abroad in other people's lands, making sure they are treated with dignity. Otherwise, the president will pull those troops out of the foreign country or change their post, position, or station, all the while protecting the troops at home. A good president will sign any legislation that will make our military proud and enable it to remain number one in the world. Our soldiers should be treated like part of the first family—first class in the nation and respected around the world. Their uniforms, their jobs, their benefits, their spouses, and their children should be cared for to the fullest extent in this country because their sacrifices for this great nation are like no other.

A good president should ensure that the US flag is respected, valued, and treated as a national treasure. The US flag represents our citizens to the world, so the citizens of this country should respect our flag because respect is reciprocal. If we respect our flag at home, then it will be respected abroad. The Red, White, and Blue waves day and night in this land—and wherever else it is spotted in the world—to tell of the glory of God and his grace to humanity. A good president who has a good signature will strongly speak out against the burning of the US flag and will support the United States in keeping our ancestors' memories alive, asking that citizens not destroy our flag, for we learn from the past. Yes, changes can be made and lessons can be learned, but some objects should be moved to a museum, not destroyed, for purposes of historical preservation and teaching. There should be stiffer penalties for people who deface or destroy important property. When looters, hiding among protesters, tried to deface the statue of the seventh president of the United States, Andrew Jackson, and demolish St. John's Episcopal Church near the White House, among other things, Trump signed an executive order to penalize anyone who laid a hand on federal property or destroyed monuments.

This reminds me of politics, campaigning, and going to the voting booth. A good president with a good signature will make sure he or she signs into law a method for free, fair, and safe elections. People should be free to talk about the candidate they want to win and be free to express their choice of candidate no matter the party the candidate belongs to, which expression is turning into a death sentence nowadays. Citizens should be free to talk about or choose their candidates privately or publicly. For some people, if others do not support the candidates of their choice, they say that it is un-American and unacceptable. We want citizens campaigning without bitterness in politics, without bitterness amid politicians, and without bitterness among the general public. The United States used to be an example to the world of a good political system, but now time has passed and change has taken place. Lately people are being attacked, having rocks thrown at them, being harassed, being called dirty words, being called racists, being insulted, being beaten, and even losing their jobs for supporting a particular candidate, things you don't expect to see anywhere in the world, even in Third World countries. This should no longer be acceptable in this country every four years at election time. Whether electing or reelecting a particular candidate, people should have the right and be free to support their platform. A good president should put in place an executive order to protect the citizens in terms of politics, elections, and voting.

People should stop choosing the president of the United States based on party. Yes, it is good to belong to a party, but it is an exceptional individual who makes a good president, not a particular party. Many people vote for a candidate because that candidate is a member of the same party, for example, Republican, Democrat, or Independent, but a US president should be selected based on capability, not on party, that is, on the qualities and character of the individual and what he or she believes he or she can do for the United States. Even then the candidate may cross party lines when choosing members of his or her cabinet. For example, a Republican presidential candidate might pick a Democrat for his or her vice president. Or a Democrat might form his or her cabinet by appointing some Republicans or Independents. Again, leadership in the United States should be based on capability, not party. That is why campaigning and debating is vital for presidential elections, so that citizens can hear what a candidate wants to accomplish for the country.

I also suggest that a good president who is equal to a good signature should change the retirement age for all Americans to fifty-seven so that Americans may have reasonable or meaningful lives after retirement, after they have worked and served their entire lives. A good president should also sign a bill to allow US citizens to become homeowners by imposing an affordable and reasonable interest rate that will not break their backs or the bank, or cause them hypertension anytime they remember the mortgage payment. Not being able to be a homeowner is indeed a very big concern in this country, and a good president will be able to solve this problem once and for all. A good president will not lead the United States into anxiety over anything, for instance, war, inflation, the economy, food scarcity, high gas and oil prices, wide-open borders and what comes with them, the future of the United States, and American children not doing well in education compared to their counterparts in other countries around the world.

Cancer is the second-leading cause of death around the world, claiming the lives of beautiful women, handsome men, beautiful children, and even babies still in their mothers' wombs, yet unborn. A good signature, which means a good president, should be able to provide a cure for cancer once and for all. Sweden leads the world in diabetes care. I wish the United States would become known for leading the world in cancer treatment and prevention.

The United States of America should welcome people from all around the world, people who have talents, gifts, and education. We should welcome them into the United States to fill the gap for us. These are the kinds of people the United States should welcome first. Let a good signature make such a thing possible, reducing or eliminating deaths from cancer and causing the United States to become known all around the world for curing cancer.

I call the United States a world power, the giant of the world, and the last bus stop. It is a country where if you have never been here, you have not even started. If you have never been to the United States, then you are missing out because the United States is freedom.

In God We Trust is the US motto. When we have a president in the White House who believes in God, it makes for perfection. Make America Great Again is Trump's campaign slogan, and he started out his first day in office by making the United States great. As president of the United States, he promised to donate his salary to charities or toward good causes. For example, he donated thousands of dollars to national parks, education, human services, and transportation, among other concerns. Ever since he took office, he has accomplished a lot. Starting with jobs, he made a promise and fulfilled it by creating around seven million new jobs, of which around six hundred thousand were new jobs in manufacturing. Some manufacturing companies had already left the country, and others were about to leave. Trump, being the greatest dealmaker of all time and a negotiator, struck deals with some of these latter companies to remain in the United States and continue their manufacturing.

When Donald Trump was president, unemployment reached its lowest point ever because he helped around one hundred fifty-seven million Americans get back to work, which also removed millions of people from SNAP (the food stamp program) for good, enabling them to stand strong on their own. Not only did Trump give us fish, but also he taught us how to catch fish. Former president Trump provided private sector training for millions of Americans, of which First Daughter Ivanka Trump Kushner was the champion. She helped with the training of people and the finding of jobs in different work areas or with other employers, for instance, Walmart, opening up job opportunities for some.

There was a massive tax cut and tax regulation,

not a tax hike, imposed by Trump that has benefited a whole lot of people in recent years, for instance, farmers, who have enjoyed a nice break from taxation of their farm produce. Manufacturing companies and almost every American under Trump's presidency benefited from a tax cut larger than any legislated by any other president in recent history. Trump ended the unfair tax known as debt tax for farmers and small businesses. He gave them hope and strength with a tax break and never a tax hike. In addition to making it possible for the United States to export its beef to the European Union and signing an agreement to lower trade barriers in Europe, Trump reduced the unfair regulations that have impacted agriculture production. He gave farmers twenty-eight billion dollars more than the relief denied them for two years, which in part was funded by the money he collected from China for not paying their fair share to the United States in the years before he became president. Trump signed trade policy to open the market for farmers to sell their produce to other countries such as Morocco, Australia, Japan, Tunisia, and China, thereby making the United States the largest producer of high-quality, hormone-free beef for export and leveling the plain field. This trade policy will help farmers and ranchers grow more than two hundred seventy million dollars' worth of crops per year and grant them market share in Europe, which encourages agriculture as a whole to produce more and to produce more sustainability.

In the grocery stores where I shop, sometimes there is not enough of certain types of produce or else certain types of produce are available only for a short time, for example, watermelon, which at certain times of year is expensive and at other times costs less and looks to be in season, but the stock doesn't last. But after Trump took office and met the needs of US agricultural producers, watermelon and other agricultural products were less expensive and also stayed around longer, so I could enjoy them as often as I wanted. They were in the market almost year-round.

Trump is the lion that protects our nation.

My tribal people call people like him *agu na eche mba*. Trump went to military school. He knows very well that the military is the backbone of every country. "If you watch out for us, we will watch out for you," he said, speaking to leaders of other nations. He loves the military, showing them respect and paying attention to all their concerns. Former president Trump rebuilt our military and finally rescued our honorable veterans who were living amid terrible conditions and whose health care was being poorly managed before he came to power. When he took office, he fixed and reformed the United States military, turning it back into what it was always supposed to be. In four years, he doubled the size of the military workforce and enabled the building of modern equipment to protect the country as needed. He introduced lasers to the military to serve different purposes and aid in job efficiency. Also, he budgeted billions of dollars per year for the Department of Defense and gave three separate pay raises to the military during his four years in the White House.

Trump restructured the military in such a way that the United States started manufacturing military equipment, weapons, and drones. Now the United States has the most accurate, most modern, and most lethal military equipment on earth, with a surplus to sell to other countries if needed, for example, Japan, Taiwan, Saudi Arabia, the United Arab Emirates, and Jordan. One piece of military equipment redesigned and manufactured on Donald Trump's watch is the tank, of which 160 mighty M1 Abrams models were built in Ohio. Engines and missile defense systems were manufactured in Alabama; F-35 fighter jets, Texas; 120 mm guns, New York and Pennsylvania; aircraft carriers, Virginia; transmissions, Indiana; and special armor, Idaho—along with drones, ships, missiles, tanks, fighter jets, and other aircraft. Trump funded the building of cyberdefense and missile defense systems, all made in the United States, and some of the highest quality in the world. The United States used some of the foregoing items whenever needed and sold some to our allies and made a profit from them, which also contributed to economic growth.

Donald Trump does not discriminate, and he believes that all military service is service no matter where a person served, whether here at home or anywhere else in the world. He recognized the Korean War and ordered that the remains of US soldiers be brought home from North Korea decades after the war ended. He also ordered brought home the remains of some World War II US Marines from Gilbert Island in the Pacific, where they had been since 1943. Trump supported gold star families by canceling the so-called widow's tax, which unfairly prevents some military spouses from receiving the full benefits earned by their beloved deceased partners. He passed Veterans Choice and Veterans Accountability. He ordered that veterans be permitted to choose their own doctors and get treatment or medical care as needed at any time from any hospital of their choice. Veteran unemployment dropped to its lowest rate after Trump took office and throughout his four years as president. He is fast and thinks faster, and that is how he knew that it was no longer business as usual, that business could be done here on earth and above in the sky, which is why he created the sixth branch of the United States Armed Forces: the space force. His administration sent two astronauts to space, and they came back within two months after years of not being able to go on that type of mission. Also, NASA launched four astronauts in a SpaceX capsule— for the first operational mission ever at Kennedy Space Center—headed to the International Space Station. On May 30, 2020, SpaceX launched astronauts from the United States, Russia, and the United Arab Emirates and transported them via the *Dragon* capsule to the International Space Station on behalf of NASA. SpaceX became the first private company to send people into orbit, and SpaceX was on the verge of becoming the first private company to bring people back from orbit after forty-five years of the Russian rocket shuttle era.

Also as a businessman, Trump knows that the

commercial space industry is the future, so he spoke in parable to the world. "You can be the first in the world while America will be number one in the world," he said. "You are number one in space, build many space suits and capsules, for America is a nation of pioneers, seventeen miles an hour."

When Trump was president, it was the first time US astronauts had been launched into space from US soil since 2011, the year of the final space shuttle flight. With Doug Hurley and Bob Behnken as astronauts, the mission took off from Kennedy Space Center's historic Launchpad 39A at 3:22 p.m. Eastern Time. President Trump, Vice President Pence, and their wives, the first lady and second lady, watched the launch from Kennedy Space Center. NASA renamed its headquarters after the first African American woman engineer at NASA, Mary. W. Jackson, on June 24, 2020. Since then, there have been other missions to space. Trump signed an executive order to forgive any moneys, even if only pennies, owed by permanently wounded soldiers in this country, in the name of more school loans, because he loves the military and veterans.

Under Trump, the United States produced the largest volume of crude oil and gas in the world, surpassing Russia and Saudi Arabia.

Donald. J. Trump is *Ekwueme*, a word from my African dialect meaning "commander in chief." He does what he says; he practices what he preaches; and he never says what he cannot do. That is the reason I call him a talk and do commander in chief. During his campaign, l observed that he had Israel in mind when he promised to move the US Embassy in Tel Aviv to Jerusalem within a five-month period. And guess what he did? He moved the embassy to Jerusalem within that time frame. He signed a proclamation recognizing Israeli sovereignty over the Golan Heights, which is critical for the settlement and security of our ally Israel. Trump also promised to move the Israeli capital from Tel-Aviv to Jerusalem in only five months, and behold, he accomplished it.

For moving the capital of Israel to Jerusalem

within five months just as promised during your campaign, and for moving the US Embassy to Jerusalem, dear President Trump, may the God of the Israelites continue to bless you and your generation.

For any African American people who are still in doubt about who Trump is, or what he thinks about us as a race, or what he has done for us, know that Trump cares for us. He accomplished so much for our people. He lifted millions of children out of poverty, and he canceled thousands of job-killing regulations that made it hard for people of color to get jobs, which also helped in creating more new jobs, including manufacturing jobs, thereby making it easier for people of color in this country to get jobs more easily; and he signed an executive order banning federal agencies from outsourcing jobs to foreign workers because it threatens the livelihoods of Americans. African American unemployment reached its lowest point in a long time under Trump's administration, and the income of African American and Hispanic people was high compared to in the past. Seventy-five percent of the new jobs went to people who had been out of the labor force. And Trump doubled the Child Tax Credit. He signed an executive order to address Chicago crime and introduced Operation Legend to help with national security and our nation's well-being at a time when we needed security most, as our children weren't even safe in their own rooms or when playing outside the house because of so many bad people with bad intentions and also because of all the gun violence. It was a violent criminal in Chicago who took the life of four-year-old LeGend Taliferro, who was shot and killed as he was sleeping in his own house. A suspect was arrested. The former president's wish for the United States is to be a violence- and crime-free country. Operation Legend, which he created, began a national crackdown on violence, with crimes including gun violence, drug trafficking, human trafficking— especially of children and women—and bank robbery. He funneled millions of dollars to the

Justice Department to aid in stopping human trafficking, especially of women and children.

Indeed, Donald Trump went to occupy 1600 Pennsylvania Avenue for the first time with the inclusion of us African American people and people of color—and all people—on his mind. The United States' first house, the White House, is a beautiful and honorable place to work, and Trump worked there with a lot of people around him, white, African American, Asian American, and Hispanic American, with the inclusion of people of color proudly, for instance United States Secretary of Housing and Urban Development Dr. Benjamin Solomon Carson, who was confirmed on March 2, 2017, and who served until January 20, 2021. Surgeon General Jerome Michael Adams is an anesthesiologist and a former vice admiral of the Commission Corps of the United States Public Health Service who served as the twentieth surgeon general of the United States from September 5, 2017, to January 20, 2021. Senator Tim Scott representing South Carolina, from 2013. The USS *Doris Miller* was named as the newest United States Navy aircraft carrier, the first time an African American service member was ever honored in such a way. Carla Hayden was sworn in as the fourteenth librarian of Congress on September 14, 2016. She is the first woman and the first African American to serve in that post, and she served under the Trump administration. When Trump was in office, he swore in the first black chief of staff of the air force, General Charles Quinton Brown Jr., the first African American to lead any branch of the United States Armed Forces. Brown served as the twenty-second chief of staff of the air force, having been confirmed by the Senate on June 9, 2020.

Under Trump, United Airlines started its first one-way nonstop direct flight UA1122 to Cape Town, South Africa, saving a whopping eight hours of travel time, which was a huge win for tourism to South Africa. In 2018 under Trump, East African Airways started its first flights into United States airspace, KQ002 and KQ003, a one-way nonstop flight from Nairobi, Kenya, to New York and a one-way nonstop flight from New York to Nairobi, respectively. Trump revoked certain housing regulations and changed the previous administration's housing regulation scheme that affected African Americans, causing racial division in the suburbs. "Education is power," Nelson Mandela said. Former president Donald Trump gave us school choice. Today, US citizens, including people of color, can send their children to the school of their choice in any zip code or district, or can now avoid sending their children to failing schools and failing systems, instead choosing the schools that have good reputations. This was accomplished by Trump's administration. Trump said that parents have the choice between charter school, private school, or homeschool. He also funneled funding to historically black colleges and universities (HBCU), committing millions of dollars annually, and he signed the Future Act and increased funding for the federal Pell Grant program. Trump ended Bill Clinton's crime policy era that affected African Americans so unfairly, the 1994 federal crime bill having been a primary driver of mass incarceration of African American men. Clinton thought he was tough on crime, but one in every three black males got caught up in the criminal justice system after the bill passed. Former president Trump did not put African Americans in jail with one policy or the other; instead he freed many African American brothers and sisters and would like to free more of them. He signed an executive order on free speech in colleges and on campuses; an executive order to fight college and campus anti-Semitism; and an executive order to expand school choice for Hispanic students, the White House Hispanic Prosperity Initiative, which gave Hispanic Americans access to educational and economic services and improved charter schools.

Donald John Trump signed a law making Dr. Martin Luther King Jr. Day a federal holiday. All that time, so many politicians were merely playing politics with us every four years, claiming to be us or to be for us African Americans, but refusing to sign legislation making Dr. Martin

Luther King Jr. Day a federal holiday. As a proud black woman, this issue is personal to me. It is said that respect is reciprocal, so I owe former president Trump my respect for respecting our own Dr. King. I would not even be in the United States, the greatest country in the world, without Dr. King's sacrifice. He did what the Lord sent him to earth to do, to preach the gospel, save lives and souls, and give freedom to humanity. Dr. King made the ultimate sacrifice. Thank you, President Trump. You are clever to have started with us African Americans by respecting our ancestors. You earned my respect in return. Many people forget easily and don't respect Trump in return, but I think it is necessary to recognize him who recognized us. Clearly he is for all people, for all Americans. Now on this federal holiday honoring Dr. King, we have enough time to do any activity we choose and have a barbecue, and still have time to sit down and listen to Dr. King's incredible speeches such as "I Have a Dream."

Trump freed many of us African Americans and wanted to free even more of us. He helped get the sentences of some celebrities and one mayor commuted. He commuted the sentence of former mayor of Detroit Kwame Kilpatrick, who was down for thirty-some years, and of sports gambler Billy Walters. Trump freed Lil Wayne, Kodak Black, and A$AP Rocky, and he pardoned Michael Flynn, Paul Manafort, Steve Bannon, George Papadopoulos, Dick Cheney, and Charles Kushner. He freed so many people that I cannot mention them all here. The Trump effect also influenced the life of Terrence Williams, who visited Trump at the White House.

In the 1980s, there was a farm whose owner was no longer be able to manage it, meaning the family's livelihood was about to fold. This family nearly lost everything and were looking forward to a foreclosure, which can lead to hunger and homelessness, but Trump stopped the foreclosure and saved the farm, the farmer's means of keeping a roof over his family's heads and being able to feed them. Another example of the Trump effect took place at the Trump Tower in the heart of New York City, where a homeless woman snuck into one of the condominiums and started living there. When the news was broken to former president Trump, his reaction was to order the people responsible for building services to feed the woman and let her stay. On his authority, the homeless woman was sheltered there in Trump Tower and fed well for close to a decade. I wonder how many billionaires would have handled the homeless woman the same way, with mercy, as Trump did, in the most expensive building to live in the world. No wonder it is said that some have taken care of angels without knowing it. Hebrews 13:1–8 reads, "Stay on good terms with each other, held together by love. Be ready with a meal or a bed when it is needed. Why, some have extended hospitality to angels without ever knowing it! Regard prisoners as if you were in prison with them. Summarily, remember to welcome strangers, because some who have done this have welcome angels without knowing it. Blessed are the merciful, for they shall obtain mercy." No one should question that the Lord has been indeed good to former president Trump.

On August 18, 2020, on the hundredth anniversary of US women's right to vote for president, Trump signed a pardon on behalf of Susan B. Anthony, who was president of the National American Woman Suffrage Association, a group dedicated to women's voting rights. After signing the proclamation of the Nineteenth Amendment on the ratification, Anthony refused to pay a fine for illegal voting in 1872 in her hometown, which got her in trouble and arrested. The woman suffrage leader was arrested for voting in her hometown of Rochester, New York, and was convicted, the conviction being widely publicized, as was the trial. President Ulysses S. Grant pardoned others, including election inspectors, but did not pardon Susan Anthony. But former president Trump did officially pardon her, the leading suffragist of her time who died in 1906, after twenty-seven other presidents did not, refusing to do so.

In 2014, members of the armed group Boko Haram kidnapped about two hundred senior girls at the Chibok Government Secondary School for

Girls in the northeastern part of Nigeria. That happened a couple of years before Trump took office, but he is the only US president who tried to rescue those girls. After a couple years, they and their families had lost hope. Some of these girls were killed by their abductors; some were raped or enslaved; and others became mothers before they could be rescued from their abductors. But they were rescued by former president Trump. When it was said that Bashar al-Assad, the president of Syria, used chemical weapons on the people of Syria, including children, President Trump did not keep quiet. He said something and did something, namely, he sent around fifty-seven missiles to Syria targeting different bases and other places. His predecessor while in office drew a red line, but it was crossed over again and again with no consequences. But Trump reacted immediately to the gas or chemical attack on Syrians, including Syrian children, whom it affected severely, some of the children having to be rushed to hospitals because they could not breathe or could not open their eyes. Former president Trump gave Assad a warning that if the chemical attacks on his people were to be repeated, then Assad would meet with serious consequences. That is what is called a US president standing tall on the world stage.

I always like the chant "USA! USA! USA!" because it brings out the power, mightiness, love, and freedom of our country, which I love. And who exemplifies these things better than Donald Trump? Trump loves his country, the United States, and despite the politicians and politics, the United States loves him too. As of today, if the United States is a big tree standing in front of us as an example. Check it very closely: there must be a Trump leaf, if not a Trump root. He is the kind of man whom one cannot bully at all. Certainly he is the kind of president or presidential candidate who cannot be bullied out of the race because he is not a career politician. In a world where Russia is flexing its muscles with regard to Ukraine, China is flexing its muscles with regard to Taiwan, and of course North Korea is flexing its muscles with regard to South Korea, among other examples around the world, the United

States of America needs a strong and intelligent president, a president who is smart, is wise, is a peacemaker, is the greatest dealmaker of all time, is flexible when making deals, and has love for this country, the United States, with all his heart. The challenging, attack, and the muscle flexing affects our allies. A world where our allies are aligning with our adversaries is a dangerous and hopeless world, as it signals our weakness to nations around the globe. And I know that this did not happen on Trump's watch. No, it needs to be fixed. Things do not look promising, because our image as a country around the world can compromise or affect our military might and trust from our allies. To have friends is better than to have enemies. Last time I checked, only one presidential candidate was talking more about friends than about foes. Last time I checked, only one presidential candidate appeared equal to the task ahead, and last time I checked, there was only one name that everyone recognized and only one candidate whom everyone listened to and respected or feared—and that was Donald Trump.

During the Trump administration, Attorney General Barr reinstated the death penalty for Dzhokar Tsarnaev, 2013 Boston Marathon bomber, who killed some people including an eight-year-old. Also, people lost their legs, hands, and other limbs in the bomb blast. When Trump said, "If you kill an American, you will be killed," he meant it. Tsarnaev's sentence of the death penalty was overturned because his attorneys said there was not enough evidence. But President Trump said that if you kill an American, you will be killed, and called for action to try the case again, saying that the bomber deserved the death penalty.

Criminal justice reform has always been on Trump's mind. He introduced and signed into law criminal justice reform, the First Step Act, that allows for the release of well-behaved prisoners and gives them a second chance in life. "Hire all Americans, including former inmates," Trump said, encouraging employers to adopt

41

second chance hiring practices. He ordered that Americans with criminal records who had served their time well be provided with opportunities. Trump declared April 2018 as Second Chance Month. Unemployment among Americans with criminal records was very high, but when Trump took office and he introduced this second chance to focus on the success and reentry into society of people with criminal records, hundreds of inmates were favored and benefited from the legislation. Trump made it possible for former inmates to secure housing, licenses to drive, and occupational licenses. He promised prison mentorship through proven programs such as Prison Fellowship, as fellowship is needed by people not in prison and those who are in prison. Trump budgeted millions of dollars to fund this reentry program. Examples of individuals who benefited from this reform are Alice Johnson, to whom Trump granted clemency following a request made by celebrity Kim Kardashian in 2018 after Johnson had served almost twenty-two years of a life sentence in prison. Matthew

Charles, who was sentenced to thirty-five years in prison, also benefited from this program. Trump's four years in the White House gave us hope, favor, forgiveness, strength, protection, recognition, and respect around the world. In 2020, under Trump's presidency, Pope Francis appointed the first black cardinal, Wilton Gregory.

Trump increased high-quality child care. In September 2020, Trump awarded a Congressional Gold Medal to Emmett Till, a fourteen-year-old black boy lynched by white men in August 1955 while visiting his cousins in Mississippi, an act that brought some degree of justice for Till. Under Trump, in 2020, the House designated lynching as a federal hate crime punishable by up to a life sentence in prison or a heavy fine, sixty-five years after Till was murdered. Honoring Emmett Till with the Congressional Gold Medal also achieved justice for the thousands of other lynching victims, most of them African Americans.

Trump signed a resolution to rename two post offices in the Los Angeles area in honor of Marilyn Monroe and Ritchie Valens. In November 2023,

Trump opened a tennis performance center in Sterling, Virginia, where he teamed up with tennis superstar Serena Williams, the two of them playing tennis as he kicked off the opening ceremonies. Trump saw record-breaking stock market performance throughout his four years in office. During his administration, the United States economy finished the year 2019 in very good shape with the Nasdaq closing at 9,000 for the first time in a long time and with the Dow closing high twenty-two times in 2019, which was made possible because of Trump's tax scheme and regulation cuts. Former president Trump signed an executive order creating a White House task force on missing slain Native Americans and Alaska Natives. On June 29, 2017, he approved a pipeline that will cross our southern border, going right under the wall from McAllen, Texas, to Reynosa, Tamaulipas, Mexico, to assist with the infrastructure needed to promote energy independence in the United States.

When President Trump took office, the opioid crisis was devastating communities across the

United States. Trump signed a bipartisan bill to fight the opioid and neonatal crises, of which our former first lady, the beautiful Melania Trump, was the champion, fighting addiction. She loves the children of the United States. Trump signed the Alexander Bill to solve the opioid crisis. He made changes on Medicare and Medicaid to pay for opioid screening and treatment so that nobody would be left behind and so that no one could make any excuses for why people could not be treated if they needed help. These changes allowed physicians to prescribe a wean-off medication for addicts. The thousands of deaths related to opioid drug overdose, including neonatal children and children born with an addiction and suffering from neonatal abstinence syndrome, reduced in number under his management. Under Trump, there was a better-regulated method for prescribing medication for opioid addiction. The number of legal opioid prescriptions was down around 23 percent. The former first lady called on lawmakers to pass a law that would allow anyone struggling with opioid use to seek help with no shame. The number of opioid prescriptions declined in 2018, and the number of opioid deaths declined for the first time in thirty years under the Trump administration.

Trump is a peacemaker. A king is born, not made. When the king supported by God rules the earth, there will be peace. Trump's wish for our country, our allies, and the whole world was for peace, love, security, and prosperity. During his campaign, Trump talked about how important peace in the Middle East was, how important peace between Israel and Palestine was, how important peace in the Korean Peninsula—North Korea and South Korea—was, and how important peace for humanity in general was. He started the peacemaking process, facilitating talks between Israel and Palestine, also recognizing the importance of moving the capital of Israel to Jerusalem. Our former president's peacemaking has reunited North Korea and South Korea, whose leaders shook hands for the first time after decades of not talking with each other and not doing business with each other. Trump did what no president had done in fifty years: recognized the Korean War, fought more than fifty years ago, and ordered that dead bodies of US soldiers be brought home from North Korea long after the war had ended. His seriousness about peace in the world, peace for North Korea and South Korea, and the denuclearization of North Korea led him to travel to Singapore and Vietnam to meet with North Korean leader Kim Jong Un and ask that peace be allowed to reign, especially in the Korean Peninsula. In the middle of the meeting, he asked the North Korean leader for total peace in the Korean Peninsula. Trump continues to engage in denuclearization talks with North Korea, even discussing denuclearization with the North Korean leader, even though he had imposed the most serious sanctions ever on them.

I am speaking from my own observations. Having observed some of Trump's accomplishments since his election and first time in the White House as president, I conclude that his performance is satisfactory. Former president

Trump was a peacemaker both at home and around the world. He decreased the tension between North Korea and the United States, which had been going on long before he took office. Before he was president, North Korea was firing off rockets with regularity, but immediately after he took office, they stopped firing rockets. Trump stepped in and made peace for the masses. Playing with rockets became a thing of the past. In 2021, Kim Jong Un tested some serious missiles such as antiship cruise missiles, which are ballistic missiles with a range of up to six hundred kilometers. He also tested new long-range cruise missiles, with a range of up to fifteen hundred kilometers, ones capable of carrying warheads. In 2022, North Korea conducted a series of tests including one in Japanese territory, which hadn't happened since 2017. North Korea fired more than a dozen missiles throughout March 2023. Rockets were flying from North Korea to South Korea like never before, up to twenty-three a day, which was a threat not only to South Korea, but also to all of humankind as it might have triggered a fight between South Korea and United States. But what a difference: under Trump's four years in power, all these activities ceased. Instead of going to war, Trump prevented the one that was almost here: North Korea.

During Trump's four years in office, there was a degree of peace between Israel and Palestine. As mentioned before, the leaders of North Korea and South Korea shook hands for the first time in decades thanks to an action of peacemaker Trump. Instead of starting a war, Trump prevented the one he almost inherited with North Korea, and prevented war between North Korea and South Korea. On February 29, 2020, in Doha, under the Trump administration, the United States and the Taliban signed a historic deal meant to end the United States' longest war, which also echoed peace to the world, not war. Around five thousand US soldiers came home after that meeting, although a few remained in Afghanistan. The Taliban and the United States agreed to a de facto seven-day ceasefire, which paved the way for two sides to sign the historic peace deal. He entered office in 2017 and vowed to end the war about which he lamented during his campaign. The Afghan American diplomat Zalmay Khalilzad, who served as United States ambassador, led the eighteen-month talks, where it was decided that if the Afghans maintained peace, cracked down on insurgents who were trying to use Afghanistan as a base for terror, and observed a permanent ceasefire within one hundred thirty-five days, then they would see a full withdrawal of US troops. But first Trump was going to reduce the number of troops from thirteen thousand to around eighty-six hundred. When he assumed office around that time, the war had taken the lives of about twenty-four hundred United States service members, both men and women, and the lives of around ninety thousand Afghans. It was worth ending, and people on both sides were happy. Surely war will never help people on planet Earth.

Trump brokered peace between Armenia and Azerbaijan, the two countries observing a ceasefire after four weeks. He once made peace between

Serbia and Kosovo and assisted the normalization of their economies, with an agreement being signed. The signing took place in the Oval Office at the White House, the signatories being Serbia president Aleksandar Vučić and Kosovo prime minister Avdullah Hoti, who signed the document in the presence of former president of the United States Donald Trump in 2020, two months before the US presidential election. The United Kingdom and Ireland struck a deal to restore the Northern Ireland government following the collapse three years before. Trump talked them into making such a resolution so as to allow peace to reign between the two countries.

I would like to see another Trump–Netanyahu collaboration because during their presidencies, which happen to take place during the same period, everyone was singing, "Peace, peace, peace, peace, peace, peace, peace on earth." Trump, for the United States of America, and Benjamin Netanyahu, for Israel, together and within less than four years nearly brought peace to the Middle East and to the whole world.

Take for instance the Abraham Accords and cancelation of the annexation of Palestine by Israel, which cancelation Trump contributed to so that Muslims and Christians could share certain important historic sites with each other and visit such places in each other's respective corners of the world, So, now Muslims can go to Israel and pray, and now the world can do business together, share ambassadors, build embassies, and visit important places in each other's lands. Christians, Hindus, Jews, Muslims, and people of other religions are all included. Trump asked to allow a Made in Israel trademark for Israeli products, also suggesting that any American born in Jerusalem should have dual citizenship (US and Israeli) designated on his or her passport. Trump's hope was that a United States passport could indicate that a citizen born in Jerusalem is from Israel.

Language was no longer a barrier for peace to take place because people were eager to communicate with each other and the world under Trump's watch in the White House. The

Abraham Accords, a statement of peace and of normalization of relations signed by Israel, the United Arab Emirates, Bahrain, and the United States of America, were signed at the White House in Washington, DC, by Bahraini foreign minister Abdull Atif Rashid al-Zayani, Israeli prime minister Benjamin Netanyahu, United Arab Emirates foreign minister Abdullah bin Zayed al-Nahya, and United States president Donald Johnson Trump as mediator. The peacemaking agreement was written in English, Hebrew, and Arabic. Peace knows no language as a barrier; all we need around the world is peace and love, which is something that former president Trump knows quite well, the proof being that no war happened under his watch or during his administration. Russia would not have invaded Ukraine, and Hamas would not have attacked Israel. Instead, countries were brokering accords, coming together, making connections, becoming friends again, and doing business again, both in the Middle East and other regions of the world.

Peace and love really reigned under former president Trump in his four years in office.

The first commercial flight from Israel to Bahrain landed in Bahrain, an island off the coast of Saudi Arabia, a week after the signing of the peace deal. After Bahrain, Sudan followed to normalize ties, being the third country to do so. Morocco was the fourth to join Israel in adopting the accord. EL AL airlines made a historic landing in Abu Dhabi, the aircraft carrying senior US and Israeli officials on the first direct commercial flight from Israel to the United Arab Emirates. following the recent signing of United States–brokered deal to normalize relations between the countries. The aircraft crossed Saudi Arabian airspace, which in the past had been blocked to Israeli traffic. Speaking at an airport ceremony, senior adviser to the Trump administration Jared Kushner, the president's son-in-law, called the event a historic breakthrough and expressed his hope that this would be the first of many such flights.

The United Arab Emirates formally ended

its commercial boycott of Israel, although the two countries had quietly conducted business for years, and was the third Arab nation to normalize its relationship with Israel and also the first Arabian Gulf country to normalize ties with Israel, after Egypt in 1979 and Jordan in 1994. On August 8, 2020, former president Trump announced the deal, saying he helped broker the accord, with Israel agreeing to suspend its planned annexation of areas of the West Bank. The agreement also firmed up opposition to regional power Iran, perhaps obstructing and reducing Iranian influence. While the United Arab Emirates, Israel, and the United States of America view Iran as the main threat to the Middle East, the United Arab Emirates (UAE) was the first Arabian Gulf country to reach a deal with the Jewish state. Israel signed peace agreements with Egypt in 1979 and with Jordan in 1994, but the UAE and most Arab nations did not recognize Israel and had no formal diplomatic or economic relationship with Israel up to this point. UAE president Sheikh Khalifa bin Zayed al-Nahyan issued a decree on August 29, 2020, authorizing Israel and Israeli firms to do business in the United Arab Emirates and permitting UAE residents to purchase and trade Israeli goods. On August 31, 2020, the first direct commercial flight operated by Israel flagship carrier EL AL landed in Abu Dhabi carrying United States and Israeli officials, including President Trump's son-in-law and senior adviser Jared Kushner. Also under Trump, Serbia and Kosovo announced normalized economic ties as part of the United States–brokered talks that included the idea of Serbia moving its embassy to Jerusalem and Kosovo recognizing Israel after two days of meetings with Trump administration officials. Serbia president Aleksandar Vučić and Kosovo prime minister Avdullah Hoti agreed to cooperate on a range of economic efforts to attract investment and create jobs. Serbia's decision to move its embassy from Tel Aviv to Jerusalem was an indication to both Israel and the United States, after the Trump administration recognized Jerusalem as Israel's capital in 2017 and moved the US Embassy in 2018, five months after Trump said he was going to do so (and after Kosovo, a predominantly Muslim country, broke away from Serbia in 2008), that it finally recognized Israel. In September 2020, Serbia and Kosovo announced restored economic ties with Israel. On September 15, 2020, Israel and the United Arab Emirates sealed the deal at the White House. Saudi Arabia welcomed the deal between Israel and the United Arab Emirates with caution, thinking that it might help stop Israel's annexation of West Bank territory as sought by the Palestinians. It was a positive thing, they said. Bahrain, Oman, and Egypt all welcomed the news and began planning to join in. Their doing so would help with the peace talks between Israel and Palestine.

The White House announced the decision of Bahrain and the United Arab Emirates to sign the peace agreement with Israel on September 15, 2020, which happened on the South Lawn of the White House. Present at the Abraham Accords signing was Abdullah bin Zayed bin al-Nahyan, United Arab Emirates foreign affairs and international cooperation minister; Abdullatif bin Rashid al-Zayani, Bahraini foreign minister; Benjamin Netanyahu, Israeli prime minister; and President Trump, all signing the declaration of peace in English, Hebrew, and Arabic. One of the purposes of the Abraham Accords was to create peace in the Middle East, stop Israel's annexation of Palestine, allow Muslims to visit the holy places in Israel, and permit all the signatories to trade together, exchange embassies, exchange ambassadors, and enable tourism.

Donald Trump, in his time in office, extended the Florida offshore oil drilling ban to South Carolina and Georgia, signing a memorandum to prohibit drilling for oil in the waters off the Florida coast and off the coast of Georgia and South Carolina for a period of ten years, from July 1, 2022, to June 20, 2032. The then extant memorandum covered the Gulf of Mexico, and the new one, in 2020, covered the Atlantic Coast and was announced in Jupiter, Florida.

Under Trump's presidency, the spying on

the United States by other countries, especially China, from land, air, and sea was put an end to. The leaving behind of Americans, especially US soldiers, in harm's way, and the leaving behind of military equipment worth of billions of dollars to waste in another land did not happen. The killing of thirteen United States service members in an attack by the Islamic State terrorist group outside Kabul's airport in Afghanistan at Abbey Gate on August 26, 2021, while the service members were helping people evacuate the country when the attack happened, would not have happened on Trump's watch. No war happened under Trump. The Ukraine war instigated by Russia would have not happened because Trump was tough on Russia.

Under former president Trump, the United States saw the future first before other countries and leaders, because Trump is a visionary and takes action immediately before other people. During the former president's administration, protesters blocking airports, the waving of other countries' flags, and the burning of the US flag was not allowed. Former president Trump's administration withdrew the United States of America from the 1992 Treaty on Open Skies with Russia a few months after Trump announced his intention to pull out of the pact. The Treaty on Open Skies allows for thirty-four member nations, including Russia, to fly unarmed reconnaissance missions over each other's territory to collect data on military forces. The United States has mentioned that Russia had been violating Open Skies for years, but no one took action upon it. Former president Trump canceled this thirty-two-year-old treaty with Russia, also withdrawing the United States from the 1987 Intermediate-Range Nuclear Forces Treaty with Russia in August 2019, leaving only the 2010 New START Treaty as the last remaining United States-Russia arms deal, which at the time had an expiration date of February 2021. Certainly the conflict between Israel and Hamas would not have happened on Trump's watch after all the help and support he gave to Israel and what he did to ISIS and its caliphate.

Vladimir Putin, the Russian president, pulled out of the last remaining nuclear arms control treaty with the United States in February 2023, saying he was suspending his country's participation in the New START nuclear arms reduction treaty with the United States. Putin made this declaration in his annual state-of-the-nation address to Russia's National Assembly, deciding to suspend the nuclear arms treaty as tension built between the United States and Russia amid the anniversary of the beginning of the Ukraine war, for which he blamed the West.

Trump also closed the Russian Nord Stream pipeline, which was one of the main sources of income for Russia, thereby making the United States energy independent. The United States had enough oil that even other countries could buy from us, and closing the Nord Stream pipeline negatively affected Russia's revenue, which in turn affected its ability to fund a war since some European countries were no longer buying oil from Russia at that time. Also, Trump sanctioned Iran as needed, imposing economic sanctions on eighteen Iranian banks. He reimposed all previously lifted sanctions, citing the "unacceptable" Iran deal. These sanctions targeted critical sectors, for instance, energy, shipping, shipbuilding, and finance. The oil sanction brought about a reduction in the number of barrels of oil produced per day, which caused a reduction in importation of Iran's oil from some countries. Trump was against this and also banned Iran from developing nuclear weapons. He does not like war, instead solving things diplomatically, probably sanctioning the hell out of anything sanctionable. Trump is the face of a warrior that blunts the knife, *ihu dike na akpu mma nko* in my dialect. Trump lamented the absence of peace around the world during his campaign, spoke of the importance of peace here in the United States and also in the Middle East and the Korean Peninsula, and fulfilled his campaign promises. When he was in office, peace reigned around the world. That was what made his administration the best in recent years—promising, excellent, and worthy of being repeated. It was a great first time as a president as Trump was respected here and abroad during his first term in office.

I know a leader when I see one, a commander in chief who will stand tall in matters affecting this country and on the world stage. When Trump was president, Americans were happy, respected, and protected again around the world, and the economy was booming. But then suddenly the invisible coronavirus, COVID-19, attacked the United States and other countries around the world. Trump refused merely to take precautions with regard to China and instead tackled the virus like the strong leader he was. He put a travel ban in place and closed down borders, first with China and second with Europe, as soon as possible to reduce the transmission of the virus to the American people, which helped in reducing the number of fatalities. Trump's opposition party called him a racist for closing the border immediately, but his taking that action early helped millions of people not to catch the virus and thereby avoid death. Other countries waited too long before they eventually closed their borders, which also helped in the slowing down of the spread of the virus once they did so. Trump rallied the vice president, doctors, virologists, nurses, and other medical experts, and he increased funding for the Centers for Disease Control and Prevention (CDC) to fight the virus. He did everything in his power to protect Americans from this emergent airborne disease called COVID-19. He quickly signed billions of dollars in aid and billions of dollars in emergency relief. He signed a bill for a loan program for small businesses and forgave certain taxes during that period for any small businesses affected, also signing a bill extending the deadline for businesses that received emergency funds through the PPP (Paycheck Protection Program) to pay those loans back. The administration deferred taxes for certain individuals affected. Also, Trump extended the IRS income deadline from April 15 to July 15 to give US citizens and the Internal Revenue Service (IRS) enough time to take care of taxes. He supported the

payroll loan program for the affected workers, and he reduced the interest rate to nearly zero until the economy renormalized. On Saturday, August 8, 2020, the former president signed four executive orders for COVID-19 economic relief. Included was (1) a payroll tax holiday for Americans earning less than one hundred thousand dollars per a year at the end of 2020, the renewal of an expired federal moratorium on evictions, and enhanced unemployment benefits; (2) the suspension of student loan payments and interest payments through the end of 2020; (3) enhanced unemployment benefits with an extra jobless benefit of four hundred dollars a week, not the six hundred dollars a week ordered by his successor—a whopping two hundred dollars more; (4) the Cares Act, passed in March 2020, which stipulated that the states would have to pay a portion of these costs. Trump truly was a president who believed in the United States first. He got things done without causing inflation.

Trump suggested easing banking rules to make things easier during the outbreak, which was occurring on cruise ships, on airlines, and in schools—all of which were closed down. He brought together federal, state, and local governments, and called on the CDC and on CVS, Walgreens, Target, and Walmart pharmacies to aid in a quick and easy takedown of the virus. He connected the Kodak supply chain for blood plasma to help manufacture the ingredients needed for a COVID-19 vaccine, and he announced the Food and Drug Administration's authorization of convalescent plasma treatment for COVID-19 patients, also signing the Right to Try law and authorizing FDA emergency use of convalescent plasma therapy after thousands of people had already been treated with it, and signing Operation Warp Speed to speed up production of a vaccine for the coronavirus. Trump also introduced telehealth to make it convenient for doctors and patients to have appointments, with telehealth allowing a patient to speak with his or her doctor or other medical professional without leaving his or her house. This enabled people to know if they needed testing for the virus or not, in order to reduce the risk or avoid contamination or the spread for the COVID-19 virus. Now, for example, on video call, a doctor can watch as a patient takes his or her own pulse. If a patient has a blood pressure monitor or thermometer, a doctor can watch while he or she checks his or her blood pressure and temperature without leaving the house, which helped prevent the spread of the virus and prevented the flooding of doctors' offices and hospitals with patients. Trump allowed for Medicare to pay for telehealth appointments with no out-of-pocket expenses.

During his time in office, Donald Trump signed stimulus relief packages to help American families, including the CARES Act, pandemic EBT for students who chose to learn remotely or stay at home, and unemployment relief. He ensured that people maintained the power of choice because when it comes to health, everybody is different. He approved visual or remote learning and in-person or in-school learning. These were his ideas because he likes the United States to be independent in terms of everything it needs. Yes,

Trump made all these things possible because of his love for the United States. He served as an example of a good commander in chief.

While in office, Trump invoked the Defense Production Act to allow General Motors, part of the private sector, to help manufacture ventilators, which the United States needed, along with masks and face shields. He said that people should not have to suffer because they were not the ones who caused the pandemic. The United States manufactured its own personal protective equipment, consisting of specialized clothing and equipment used by doctors, nurses, and the masses, to protect against this infectious disease. In terms of ventilators and other materials, Trump charitably distributed these as a gesture of goodwill to foreign countries that needed them and also to help fight this virus across the globe.

Trump was taken by Marine One to Walter Reed Army Medical Center when he contracted to COVID-19, doing so only to exercise caution. He walked on and off the helicopter showing great strength, saluting the people who were waiting for their beloved president with his head up, not showing any sign of weakness, and waving his hand as always. This happened about thirty-two days before the election—another example of showing strength and leadership as commander in chief.

To aid our economic recovery, on August 8, 2020, Trump signed an executive order deferring payroll taxes, extending unemployment benefits, and postponing student loan payments. He also signed four executive orders to help the economy and citizens and to lower drug prices by opening trade between United States and other countries with cheaper prices on imported medicines. The savings went straight to patients, for example, users of insulin or EpiPens, and not to middlemen. Insurance companies were made to cover preexisting conditions. Trump took on Big Pharma and lowered the cost of prescriptions. To make sure everything necessary was done, he signed an act ordering transparency in health-care prices. He also gave orders for the use of two special ships: (1) the United States Navy hospital ship *Comfort*, which arrived in New York Harbor with one thousand beds and enough physicians to help with treating coronavirus (but it took only patients who had not come into contact with the coronavirus, to help ease the tensions of surgery) and (2) the United States Navy ship *Mercy*, which arrived in Los Angeles to help ease tensions brought about by the same situation (but it ended up taking only patients who had not come into contact with the coronavirus, to help ease the tensions of surgery).

The United States of America and the American people represent the most generous nation in the world when it comes to foreign assistance. The United States was on the front lines fighting against Ebola and influenza and supported other countries in the battle against HIV and AIDS (acquired immune deficiency syndrome), tuberculosis, and malaria. Former president Trump drove the global response to COVID-19 even as we battled it here at home in the United States. Trump wants the United States of America to be independent of everything. That is the reason he commanded that the United States to manufacture its own protective materials—ventilators, gowns, masks, gauges, respirators, and other vital equipment—to fight against the coronavirus. His administration offered ventilators to African countries fighting the virus. He pledged millions of dollars in foreign aid to other places at risk of this disease, not only African countries such as Algeria, Botswana, and the Republic of Congo, but also India and some other countries. The funds his administration provided went to support these countries by providing protective services. In the effort to fight against the coronavirus and the COVID-19 pandemic, former president Trump supported nations around the world, including Nigeria, by donating ventilators. Trump assured these countries that the United States of America stood in solidarity with Nigeria during that difficult time and extended his regards to the people of Nigeria, which gesture the Nigerians were very appreciative of. There is no doubt that the American people are the greatest humanitarians the world has ever known, and Trump proved this yet again during that trying time of coronavirus disease.

Former president Trump is a wonderful father with a wonderful family. Believing in the United States and family first, he signed a bill for paid family leave so that families could bond with their newborn children. He also protected the unborn. A prolife president believing that life starts at the time of conception, Trump passed a law and gave us the right to try a drug that might possibly cure disease, which has saved many lives. The right to try has led to some cures for cancer and other diseases, healing people who otherwise would be dead by now. Trump condemned and forbade the chaining of women in prison during childbirth. President Trump signed a bill extending compensation for victims of 9/11 eighteen years after the attack, these families nearly have lost their compensation. He fought hard and won, reinstating benefits for victims of that tragedy. In November 2019 on Thanksgiving Day, Trump visited Kabul, Afghanistan, a site not far from combat action—the day when troops most likely think about their children, spouses, siblings, parents, and friends. As a good commander in chief, he showed up, surprising the troops, making them feel warm, loved, respected, and appreciated and making them proud of being who they were—US soldiers—and thankful. He cared for American families, ensuring that no household with newborn babies would have to panic or suffer amid the shortage of baby formula or shortage of amoxicillin, an antibiotic for babies, which posed a danger to the leaders of tomorrow, that is, our babies. Wanting the United States to be independent of many things, Trump made the United States become independent in terms of steel, independent in terms of oil, and independent in terms of ventilators. There was no supply chain problem, no transportation or gas problem, and no food problem because Trump funded the farms and equipped them well, having a very good understanding of his job. And Trump rallied the CEOs of grocery stores and shopping centers, and of Walmart, Walgreens, Target, and

Costco, and met with them regularly to regulate food quality, food prices, food quantity, good salaries for workers, and distribution, and to find ways to boost the economy and the well-being of the people in this country.

A program begun under the Trump administration trained the highest number of women ever in business. On Trump's watch, a large number of women were accepted by the military, and under his administration, there was the highest number of women in Congress compared to recent years. In the seventy-second session of the General Assembly of the United Nations, Trump mentioned the empowerment of women and encouraged this movement. He told the United Nations that he was calling for the reawakening of nations for the revival of the people in terms of spirit, pride, and patriotism, and he really wanted to engage women.

Former president Trump's predecessor emphasized his concern that the greatest threat to the United States was North Korea, saying that war was imminent. There were some US citizens held hostage in North Korea, including Otto Frederick Warmbier from Ohio, the son of Frederick and Cindy Warmbier. Otto was a young American college student who died in 2017 after being imprisoned and tortured in North Korea. He went for an adventure and came back in a coma, in a vegetative state. He was sentenced to fifteen years of hard labor in 2016 after being convicted of attempting to steal a propaganda poster during a trip to Pyongyang. Former president Trump is a man of integrity. He has wisdom; he is the greatest dealmaker of all time; his is the face of a warrior that blunts the knife; and he works with flexibility. He rescued and brought home Otto, who died at the age of twenty-two in June 2017, shortly after he was brought home. Who knows without former president Trump if the United States would have recovered his body. It broke Trump's heart to hear about the death of this boy. He had to mention and honor Otto during his 2018 State of the Union Address. May the gentle soul of Otto Warmbier continue to rest at the right hand of the Lord.

This is an example of leadership through strength and power. I believe Otto would have not died if former president Trump had been in power when he was captured. I assume Otto would have not died because under Trump, missiles and rockets were no longer flying everywhere, nuclear testing had stopped, some other hostages had been released, and some military facilities were closed and already dismantled, and he ordered that the remains of our military members return home to be laid to rest in the land of the United States.

Millions of people fled Venezuela because of its socialist and communist system, which does not work. Trump sanctioned the Venezuelan president Nicolás Maduro and some among his inner circle and his close advisers. Trump announced a United States–Mexico trade agreement and a brand-new United States–Korea trade deal because, he said, people brought their products to the United States of America to sell but never reciprocated, that is, never let the United States do the same thing in their country—so, a fair trade deal made sense.

So many things Trump accomplished that I just cannot remember them all. I've mentioned only the ones I can remember at this time. In any event, Trump exceeded expectations by making good progress on his campaign promises. To undo burdensome regulations that made dishwashers slow and weak, he introduced a new and affordable dishwasher that does an excellent job in under an hour. He introduced a lifetime light bulb and also a full-flow showerhead. He helped California by not diverting water from the state, instead Trump signing an order diverting water to California regions where farming had been totally eliminated by the federal government against state wishes. He stopped robocalls that disturb people in their homes and cause them problems and stress. Trump opened the largest protected forest in the United States, which had been blocked since 2001, to the logging industry and also signed an agreement to plant one billion trees. He signed some billions of dollars in aid after the Puerto Rica hurricane and helped Bahamas with their disaster. He gave aid to Venezuela and also to Ukraine. He called out Maduro, the president of Venezuela, and the leaders of neighboring countries to urge them to recover their freedom and restore their democracy. During Trump's time in the office, Cuba nominated its first prime minister in forty years. Three former Soviet Union countries received a helping hand of many dollars in military aid—Estonia, Latvia, and Lithuania. Trump called the attention of Crown Prince Mohammed bin Salman to what happened to Jamal Khashoggi and made sure Jamal Khashoggi, a resident of the United States and a *Washington Post* columnist/journalist, got his justice. The Saudi court sentenced five individuals to death for directly participating in the murder of Khashoggi, and three other individuals were handed prison sentences totaling twenty-four years of incarceration for covering up this crime and violating the law. Three were found not guilty. That is, all the people who contributed to Khashoggi's death were sentenced in a Saudi court of law.

Under Trump, the United States manufactured

steel. "A country that does not produce steel is not a country," he said. Nowadays, the United States produces and uses some of its own steel to repair some of our infrastructure and for new construction. This saves a lot of money—plus we make money by selling steel that is produced in the United States to other countries around the world. A lot of products made in the United States are on the market today because Trump encouraged people to invest in this country and to manufacture products here, making use of the four words "Made in the USA."

Trump rescued miners who had been forgotten for years before he took office. Under Trump's administration, miners and mining came back to life and became a thing again. Miners got their careers and the jobs they loved so much back and began to take care of their families again. The United States became the largest producer of crude oil and gas in the world. Oil and gas production was better than ever, surpassing Russia and Saudi Arabia. During the Trump administration, gasoline was at its lowest price in the longest time, around $1.89 a gallon, compared to the recent price in California and some other states of $8.00 from September 2022 to November 2022. People have to go far and wide in search of gas and eventually end up buying expensive fuel.

Because of the change in administration, once Trump was no longer in office, the United States lost its ability to be the number one oil producer in the world and made it onto the list of the countries low in oil production, tapping our oil reserves that are meant for emergencies and asking for oil from other countries when we were better off when it comes to oil production before, trying to cause a misunderstanding with the Organization of the Petroleum Exporting Countries (OPEC) and Saudi Arabia. Trump supported fracking, oil drilling, and coal mining, which also helped the United States become and remain the largest producer of oil and gas throughout his time in office. He provided stable and good-paying job opportunities to the workers in these industries, along with benefits, until his successor took over. Trump signed an order on the right to pray in public (encouraging religious liberty) and signed an executive order to protect people with preexisting medical conditions from increased health insurance premiums. Trump issued a major disaster declaration for Louisiana, signed an emergency declaration for Iowa to receive federal help to recover from a windstorm that affected the corn crop, and helped California with the wildfires. He gave North Carolina a helping hand to recover from Hurricane Dorian. Trump built the mighty Hoover Dam. In the Oval Office, Trump signed the go-ahead order to begin construction on two oil pipelines that had been stopped during the previous administration, the Keystone XL pipeline and Dakota Access pipeline.

Donald Trump proved he was a Christian in many ways. Some people wanted the motto In God We Trust to be removed from our currency, but Trump preserved this important tradition of faith for our country. He kept churches exempt from paying taxes, although some people wanted to revoke this tax-exempt status. Trump never used the Internal Revenue Service as a political weapon to attack churches and other such organizations. Under Trump, the PMI (Purchasing Managers' Index) went up for manufacturing industries, and new home sales went through the roof, whereas currently people are barely buying houses. The Johnson Amendment is a provision in the United States tax code that has prohibited all 501(c)(3) nonprofit organizations, such as universities and churches, from endorsing or opposing political candidates since 1954. Former president Trump signed an executive order to defend freedom of religion and freedom of speech for the purpose of easing the First Amendment restrictions. He stopped the Johnson Amendment from interfering with pastors' right to speak their mind. He attended West Point graduation and attended the first Army-Navy game at West Point in New York since 1943. He declared a state of emergency after Tropical Storm Isaias hit the state of New Jersey.

Trump would not put the United States in danger of using its own oil reserves at the wrong time. He proposed about seventy-five million barrels of oil from oil companies to fill the reserve.

Trump exceeded his campaign promises, to which the world will testify. Norwegian lawmaker Christian Tybring-Gjedde was the first of two Norwegian lawmakers to nominate Trump for the Nobel Peace Prize in 2018. Tybring-Gjedde nominated him for his efforts to bring reconciliation and broker relations between the United Arab Emirates and Israel. That was unique and was a big deal, opening up the possibility of peace in the Middle East, which made a positive impact in the Middle East and around the world. He also made peace between North Korea and South Korea. Tybring-Gjedde added that Donald Trump met the criteria. Trump was nominated for the third time for the Nobel Peace Prize by Australian lawmaker David Flint during the first presidential debate of 2020. Citing Trump's role in helping broker relations between Israel and the United Arab Emirates, he called it the Trump Doctrine, uniting the Arab states and Israel.

On Friday, August 21, 2020, at the White

House, a memorial service and wake was held for Robert Trump, the brother of former president Trump, who died on August 15, 2020, at the age of seventy-one. Donald Trump said, "Robert is not only my brother but [also] my best friend." Trump was expected to accept his nomination for president at the Republican National Convention as he made his speech on the South Lawn of the White House. He misses his brother so much. May Robert Trump's gentle soul rest in peace.

Under the Trump administration, the economy was booming, the United States was respected around the world again, manufacturers were doing well, American workers were producing products made in the United States, the infrastructure was being repaired with materials made in the United States, and we had a surplus that we sold to the world, which also generated revenue and helped with economic growth. Former president Trump was a president with an edge. He signed a bill that made it easier for the United States to export beef into European Union, which opportunity beef farmers and ranchers have not had for a long time. He lowered the trade barrier for our ranchers, giving them leverage to export and sell to other countries, for instance, Japan, Australia, Tunisia, Morocco, and China. The United States and Japan negotiated bilateral business deals under Trump. For the previous sixteen years or so, no such negotiation had happened with no deals being brought to the table. During Trump's first time in office, the United States gained access to the Japanese market for the first time since 2003. In 2018, Japan was one of the top purchasers of large amounts of defense equipment made in the United States of America. Taiwan is also a big purchaser of military equipment made in the United States, as is Poland, who bought fighter jets costing billions of dollars from the United States. Again, this was big-time progress under the Trump administration as he improved manufacturing in the United States. Trump signed a bill allotting billions of dollars to Boeing to manufacture the F-15EX fighter jet because the F-15EX carries more weapons, and more modern weapons, including hypertonic, to replace the older F-15E jet, which was either retired or flown less frequently, having been extensively used in the wars in Afghanistan and Iraq, which was quick thinking the likes of which is expected of an excellent commander in chief of a country like the United States. Before Trump took office, the United States lost around sixty factories in twelve years, and while he was in office, the United States gained around twelve factories in three years. Former president Trump withdrew Americans from the Iran trade deal and nuclear deal—a trade deal that benefited our allies, for example, Mexico and Japan, but not us. After withdrawing the United States America from the Iran nuclear deal in 2015, he reimposed nuclear sanctions, saying that the deal favored only the Iranian leaders and that it allowed use of the funds to build nuclear-capable missiles and to fund terrorism in Syria and Yemen. Economic pressure and sanctions were imposed on Iran to deny them money from oil, clean coal, and natural gas so that the regime may not fund its needs or support its bloody agenda. Trump called on countries that bought Iranian crude oil to stop their purchases, saying, "We cannot allow the chief sponsor of terrorism to possess the planet's most dangerous weapon. We cannot allow a country that chants, "Death to America" and "Death to Israel" the ability to deliver a nuclear warhead to any city on earth." Also Trump said that the Iran deal could not protect Israel, as Trump was for Israel, our ally. Trump stopped the bad deal with China and renegotiated a fair trade deal to benefit both the United States and China. He suspended China's economic independence and also stopped Chinese students from doing research in the United States in light of the long-standing allegation that Chinese authorities were using those student researchers to collect our intellectual property. He secured entry into university research because China sends more students to United States universities than it does to colleges in any other nations. Trump terminated the United States' membership in WHO (World Health Organization) because it mismanaged the COVID-19 crisis. The World

Health Organization recommended that healthy people do not always need to wear masks. The United States paid its dues, around four hundred million dollars yearly, whereas China and other countries paid only a little. Trump said that those funds would be redirected elsewhere to other urgent global needs. Trump accused the WHO of not moving quickly enough to sound the alarm about COVID-19 and for being too China-friendly. Trump was against WHO for advising the United States of America not to ban travel from China to other parts of the world in the middle of the coronavirus outbreak, which happened to be the smartest decision because that fast movement to close the border helped a lot in reducing the number of coronavirus casualties. Other countries ended up closing their borders, but later. Trump said the World Health Organization was slow to respond and that they missed the call, adding that they should have called it months earlier. He ordered revocation of section 230 of the Communications Decency Act on Twitter (now X) because one of his tweets was removed two days after Twitter flagged it and cracked down on his tweeting.

The United States' forty-fifth president was respected everywhere he visited in the world, countries such as Saudi Arabia, England, Japan, South Korea, North Korea, India, and China. Trump was the first US commander in chief to set foot onto North Korean soil in decades. Former president Trump is flexible, and as a president needs such flexibility to strike deals, prevent wars, and work well with allies and adversaries. His flexibility is the reason he got along with North Korean chairman Kim Jong Un. He is capable of working with our allies and our adversaries alike. Trump was the first president of the United States to cross the military demarcation line in North Korea at the demilitarized zone to resume talks on the denuclearization of North Korea. The people of India respected, celebrated, welcomed, and loved him and his administration. Trump's fans in India were madly in love with him. Some of them nearly worshipped him and his status, celebrating him with songs and prayers.

A GOOD SIGNATURE

He visited India in for an event called Namaste. My favorite part of that visit was during the time for flower crafts, or you might call it a flower celebration, when the president and first lady decorated a flower bed with beautiful assorted brightly colored flowers. In China, too, there were beautiful flowers everywhere they visited. Maybe the presence of the most beautiful model God ever created, our former first lady, the beautiful Melania Trump, contributed to this. I enjoyed seeing those beautiful flowers.

In Sept 2017, President Trump and First Lady Melania led a moment of silence for the remembrance of those lost on 9/11 at the White House. The First Lady hosted a White House Kitchen Garden Event, which she invited a group of young boys and girls to help her to harvest and plant vegetables on the beautiful garden at the White House. She encouraged them to eat a lot of fruits and vegetables as a big believer in eating healthy. She asked them if they have a garden at home and what's their favorite vegetable, which they mentioned different types of vegetables, carrots, broccoli, anis, spinach, corn, string beans, and tomatoes. She told them vegetables are needed for healthy eating and she encouraged them to carry the habit on. She also read to the children in the White House during the Easter Celebration. She was given an American red carpet welcome in Ghana, people performed dances, and she visited the children because of her love for children. They showed her around the place, and showed her the gate of no return, where slaves went through and never returned. The First Lady stood there for a moment of silence, and then showed a heartfelt sympathy for those that lost loved ones through that gate.

Former president Trump went to Singapore for the Singapore Summit in 2018, and Cambodia for a peace meeting, seeking peace and security for our country and around the world. He always received a very warm presidential welcome. Lots of countries wanted to work with him, countries stretching out their hands for friendship, business, and other opportunities. He always stood tall and tough but remained pure in heart. During

Trump's first term in the White House, God gave us not only a president, but a lion that protected the nation (my African people would say *agu na eche mba*), a man who was smart and clever. All these jobs were done in little time, two to three years. And this is just to mention but a few accomplishments of the former president, as I do not remember all of them, but they mostly occurred in his first year in office, before all the political mudslinging and the witch-hunt and bullying started, for example, the Russia hoax, which Trump's enemies knew were mere allegations and not the truth, but they refused to acknowledge that the story was a false one. Then came the first impeachment trials of the forty-fifth president of the United States of America, which began in December 2019, with charges of abuse of power and obstruction of Congress, and lasted two months. All Republicans objected to the allegations with two or three Democrats objecting to both the charges. In the end, Trump was acquitted by the United States Senate and remained in the office of the president of the United States.

Donald Trump was impeached for the second time in January 2021. Very few presidents had been impeached by the House, but Trump was impeached twice—two impeachments out of the four total impeachments instigated by the House, the other two being of two previous presidents. Charged with incitement to insurrection with a trial that lasted about a month, Trump was again acquitted by the United States Senate.

When Trump called the president of Ukraine, he was criticized. He accomplished a great deal, but people were quick to criticize him. Trump is not the type of man you can bully, not the type of former president you can bully, and certainly not the type of presidential candidate you can bully. My people used to call the kind of man he is *anu ana agba egbe ona ata nri*, meaning an animal that is being shot at and it kept grazing food.

I am calling on young people, every one of you. You have been busy with studying, learning, researching, taking exams, working, and following politics, but I want you to know one thing: Trump was sent by God to open your eyes to the possibility of a brighter future, a future where you are ready at all times to tackle any circumstances, seize any opportunity, and see for yourself if Trump fulfilled his campaign promises. His wish for you is that you do well. For school choice, long-term funding for HBCUs, and free speech, the former president signed executive orders protecting our colleges and campuses and making sure every American is free in this land of freedom to speak their mind. He signed an order on the right to try, which has helped cure diseases, for example, some types of cancer. He provided high-speed internet to rural areas, provided clean air, cracked down on censorship of social media, and instituted work protection for LGBTQ persons. Under the Trump administration, employers were prohibited from firing workers because they were gay or transgender, as doing so violates Title VII of the Civil Rights Act of 1964, which prevents employers from discriminating against employees on the basis of race, sex, color, religion, or national origin. Under the Trump administration, the Supreme Court approved work protection for LGBTQ persons and the interest rate was cut by the Fed, reaching the lowest point ever during his first time in office. When he said America first, he meant it. Trump was high class in everything he accomplished. His leadership to the world brought security, prosperity, and friendship. He sanctioned Russia for interfering in the 2020 US presidential election and also gave aid to Ukraine. Trump canceled a thirty-two-year-old treaty with Russia, which tried to prevent the United States from being a world power by preventing the development of a ground-based missile with a range of five hundred to fifty-five hundred kilometers. Trump canceled the arms treaty with Russia because Russia had violated it for years. "We are not letting Russia violate nuclear weapons," Trump said. He imposed sanctions on Russian oil trading firms in order to shrink the Russian economy and also stop the cash flow to the Venezuelan regime that was behaving poorly, which caused Venezuelans to relocate, migrating to other countries because for them under President Nicolás Maduro, there was no food, no circulation of money, and insecurity, which was very concerning. During Trump's time in the office, national security was very tight. I am praying, now that Trump is not in office, that China does not frustrate the United States, threaten the United States, size up the United States, or eat the United States lunch as Trump lamented it would during his campaign. Now a Chinese weather balloon has flown into our country, spying on our military on land, in the sea, and in the sky. China's spy balloon gathered information from multiple military sites despite attempts to block it, one report said. The Chinese spy crane was part of the most wide-ranging penetration of the United States in history, the report said. I believe that China was sizing up the United States on a level I have not seen in recent years.

Recently China provoked the United States at sea when one of its warships had a close call with a United States destroyer, and it provoked the United States in the air when one of its planes cut off a United States aircraft. My preference is that China or Russia will not take the United States' position in the world, which is to be the number one at all times, in other words, the world power. It has now been four years since Trump left office. Is there any treaty that needs to be canceled, and if so, who is capable of doing it—and doing it very fast and right like Trump, so that the United States will always be safe and maintain its position as the world power, as there is no second position for the United States, it is not in Americas' genes.

Trump signed an executive order in July 2020 to hold China accountable for oppressive actions against Hong Kong. The bill imposes sanctions on any entity that helps violate Hong Kong's autonomy. Trump ordered the Chinese Consulate in Houston,Texas, to close down in order to protect American intellectual and property. He cited that American business can be done here in the country or up above in the sky. Remember space force? He sent two astronauts to space, and they came back in two months. Whether for two months or two weeks, Americans can go to space, do their business, and come back down to earth. When Trump was president, the first United States *Mariner* spacecraft in ten years lifted off from US soil, with a NASA/SpaceX crew, making history. The United States used to pay a lot to send astronauts to space, but now we have our own transportation there and no longer have to pay others, saving all that money. "A nineteen-hour trip to heaven looks heavenly," Trump said.

As a staunch Christian, Trump also reminded us to trust in God Almighty with all our hearts and to be proud of who we are as Christians. Trump reminded us to start saying "Merry Christmas" again during the Christmas season because people had dropped the tradition and were saying "Happy holidays." While every other religion names its holidays when extending such greetings, we can proudly say "Merry Christmas" again. Personally, Christmas is my favorite holiday and my happiest season of the year. I can easily flow into the mood of Christmas and forget my sorrows and worries until next year. With people saying "Happy holidays" instead of mentioning Christmas, it created a void, but when Trump came into office, he revived the saying of "Merry Christmas," which I know Christians here at home and around the world appreciate a great deal. The revenue of people who sell Christmas decorations, both real and artificial, went up the year when Trump took office. Revenue from real Christmas trees went up about 20 percent, and revenue of artificial trees went up about 12 percent after Trump said, "We will say 'Merry Christmas' again." Sometimes we must ignore politics and political practices and tactics and look for the truth. Donald Trump is a Christian star, a Christian warrior for all the Christians here at home and around the world. On December 21, 2020, a rare star showed up, the star of Bethlehem, which shone when Jesus was born. The star appeared again in a rare sighting under president Trump, an ambassador of Christ, a true

Christian former president of United States. This star was seen eight hundred years ago, and it will not appear again until 2080, one report said. Let us enjoy this rare and important gift of our former president one more time. All the campaign promises Trump made when coming down the golden escalator and formally announcing his run for the presidency on June 16, 2015, with a campaign rally and a speech lasting less than an hour at Trump Tower in New York City, he either fulfilled and exceeded. Some of the things he achieved he did not even mention during his campaign. For his first four years as president, he practiced what he preached.

Former president Trump does not like lawlessness because it breaks and destroys cities, states, and the whole country. He believes in the rule of law, respecting the US flag and what it stands for. Trump nominated three judges to the Supreme Court. His first nominee was Neil Gorsuch, his second nominee was Brett Kavanaugh, and his third nominee was Amy Coney Barrett, all three of whom were approved to be justices of the Supreme Court of the United States during the four years of his first term in the White House. Under Trump, Congress confirmed many district judges and circuit court judges. Under his leadership, Congress also upheld the Second Amendment, the right to bear arms. Citizens whose minds are healthy have the right to protect themselves or be protected. Trump supported all these measures to make sure the Constitution and law of this land were interpreted properly as written. Trump supported the men and women of all police forces because part of their job is to make sure there is law and order and security in the country. "The overwhelming majority of police are noble, courageous, and honorable," he said. So, while others sought to defund the police, he supported the police. He did not support defunding the police, instead reforming the police if there was a need. He preached that Americans should give the men and women of the police force the respect they deserved, adding that they do a good job if they are allowed to do their jobs. He emphasized that we should not take legal protections away from the police.

George Floyd was an African American man who died in police custody. A white police officer knelt on his neck for some minutes, and he died at the officer's hands on Memorial Day, May 25, 2020, in Minnesota. African Americans cried out against this wrongful death and demanded the defunding of the police. They got justice, but the former president made it clear that there would be no defunding of the police but, instead, reform. He signed an executive order on June 16, 2020, on police reform, banning the chokehold except in cases where an officer was in real danger, and also tracking misconduct by police officers. He ended the catch and release method of his predecessor as a solution to immigration and ended the ISIS caliphate 100 percent. Trump abandoned the previous administration's subsidy that funded Planned Parenthood, being one of the most pro-life presidents of all time. On August 25, 2020, President Trump participated in the naturalization ceremony of five individuals during the Republican National Convention (RNC). The five individuals naturalized were from Bolivia, Lebanon, India, Sudan, and Ghana.

"America first" is always on Donald Trump's mind. Included in the things he said during his 2016 presidential campaign are "I want to pay back my country"; "I will be your president"; "There is no room for small results"; "You have nothing to lose"; "I will beat the hell out of ISIS"; "China will not eat your lunch"; "That is a potato, and that is a peanut"; "Buy American and hire American"; "Three words: 'Made in USA'"; "Make America great again"; and "Walls and wheels work." With these words, Trump emphasized his strength to the American people, showing that he had the ability to be a good president, if not the best. And yes, he accomplished more than he promised and more than I expected. All the things he spoke of came to pass, perhaps because he was not previously a politician. There was change during his first term in office. Citizens of this country were being paid back. Indeed, they were enjoying the fruits of their labor in this land in many ways.

There was an economic comeback when Trump took office, which broke a record held for decades. People easily forget that the gross domestic product grew, beating expectations; the economy was booming; and the country was moving in the right direction with the best wages in decades. Once an economy builder, always be an economy builder. Trump is an economy grower and an economy builder. Under his administration, we had a healthy economy with no inflation.

My people say that there is a certain kind of eye that is to be feared, in my dialect *anya ana aso*. If former president Trump is an eye, then he is the kind of eye that should be feared. Some kids are not messed with by other kids, and some teenagers are not messed with by other teenagers. It is the same thing with adults: there are some adults whom other adults do not mess with. Former president Trump ordered the release of all US hostages and prisoners, both political and nonpolitical, who were being held all around the world. His foreign hostage release policy was well received. The families of hostages were pleased with the responsiveness of Trump's administration. About fifty-eight hostages were released from about twenty-two different countries around the world. The release of three American hostages from North Korea in May 2018, which looked impossible at that time, was important and remarkable for Trump. He saw it as a victory over the Democrats and his predecessor in the White House. He freed detainees and three UCLA basketball players from China. American pastor and teaching elder of the Evangelical Presbyterian Church Andrew Craig Brunson was held hostage in Turkey for two years, and Trump negotiated his release. Under Trump, Caitlan Coleman was rescued along with her family after they had been held in captivity by the Taliban for five years, In October 2012, Caitlan Coleman was about six months pregnant and was traveling through Maidan Wardak Province, Afghanistan, with her husband, as they had gone there to hike. They were kidnapped by militants, and while in captivity, Coleman gave birth to three children, making it a family of five. Joshua Holt was released from a Venezuelan jail. Danny Burch was released from a Yemen prison. Trump freed two Western hostages in Afghanistan in a deal with the Taliban—an American, Kevin King, and an Australian, Timothy Weeks, were released from an area of southern Afghanistan heavily controlled by the Taliban, ending their more than three years of captivity. They were abducted outside the university in Kabul, where both of them had been professors. In the Iran prisoner swap, Trump negotiated the release of an American, Mr. Wang, whom Iran thought was a spy but who was a Princeton student. The foregoing are but a few of the hostages and prisoners released by the Trump administration.

Donald Trump stands tall at all times on the world stage. In Syria, former president Trump confronted President Assad for using chemical weapons on Syrians, which led to health problems and the deaths of many people, including children.

Trump issued a serious warning to Assad, the Syrian leader, saying that if he used chemical weapons against his own people again, Trump was going to react appropriately to such an evil act. He sent about fifty-seven missiles to different places in Syria as a warning of what was to come if Assad abused his power again.

Also, Trump bombed the hell out of ISIS with a so-called mother bomb. That was the beginning of the end for ISIS with their bad roots and their atrocities. Some people who were helping ISIS were captured. They were tired of ISIS's bad behavior and begged to go home to their various countries.

When Trump was President, the United States was calm and the world was calm and peaceful again. I remember that before Trump took office, people were afraid to move around the country or travel to other countries as terrorism was at a high level with bomb attacks on airports. People traveling by air were not safe, and people traveling on land were not safe. People were afraid to travel even during Thanksgiving because it was not safe out there, which prevented them from visiting loved ones and their extended families. Children were not able to enjoy going door to door for Halloween candy because of this insecurity. I'm not a big fan of Halloween, but I donate candy to my kid's school and also have candy at home for my household and for the who knock at my door. I do this because it does not feel good when children come to my door and I have no candy to offer. But the last Halloween before Trump took office, the children did not come because of the insecurity here in this country and around the world. As a very emotional person, I felt very bad, almost to the point of tears, asking myself where we were headed as a country if even children in the land of the free could no longer enjoy their freedom. That was a period when no parent wanted to risk the safety or life of their children, so they kept their children from going outside the house. But because Trump has the face of a warrior that blunts the knife (as my tribal people will call it, *ihu dike na-akpu mma nko*), he promised to eliminate Isis, and indeed he stopped Isis and put an end to their atrocities and to the insecurity. There was security again here in our country and around the world immediately after he was sworn in to office. People had stopped enjoying traveling before he took office, but they immediately started enjoying traveling right again after he took office. If one compares the two Thanksgivings before Trump took office and the two Thanksgivings after Trump took office, one will surely see the difference between the two leaders and the two seasons. One will find out that people were indeed free again, that they celebrated Halloween again, and that they happy and they traveled again for Thanksgiving, Christmas, and other holidays. The United States was safer under Trump's presidency because he ensured security and order at home and around the world. During his first four years in the White House, people traveled at any time and anywhere without fear of anything. Money was circulating. During holidays, people felt at ease in their hearts. Kids could freely go door to door on the hunt for Halloween candy again because there was now security, law, and order.

Trump created ICE, a security agency helping to control the border and illegal immigration, stopping the practice of letting people from other countries into this country without proper vetting. He ended asylum for all people because some of the people seeking asylum here had evil intentions; the border was tightly secured, as was the country. He invoked Title 42, which allowed immigrant asylum seekers to stay in Mexico until they were thoroughly vetted, so that the United States of America would be able to know who was coming into our beautiful country, for example, which country a person was coming from and if the person had a history of being a terrorist, human trafficker, drug trafficker, gun trafficker, rapist, or some other type of criminal. We would also be able to know the reasons these people wanted to come to the United States, determine how many people we would be able to take care of at one time, and make sure we were not letting our enemies or people with bad intentions—for example, gang members, murderers, rapists, drug traffickers, human traffickers, or terrorists—into our country. Trump signed legislation to prevent child trafficking. During his first four years in office, the United States had the strongest border. Under him, the United States was a great nation with Trump not taking his eyes off being first in the world. Under Trump, the United States was respected again.

America, dear, you will always be the greatest. I will continue to love you and never cease to pray for you, the country that has given me freedom. I want to live in a country that is not looked upon as a joke but that is respected at home and around the world. As of November 2023, what was happening at the border showed disrespect of the US border and was an invasion of our country by immigrants. I do not blame all the immigrants, just those who are putting the lives of our border agents in danger, for instance, by throwing rocks at them or causing the agents to die untimely. One agent jumped into the Rio Grande to save one migrant's life. Some agents are shot to death or get hurt in one way or another. Such things can only happen in a country whose government does not pay attention to its borders, or if the border is simply wide open. With Trump's implementation of Title 42, the policy for remaining in Mexico that he himself introduced, people from Central America looking for asylum or hoping to migrate to the United States were able to remain in Mexico until they were thoroughly vetted before being cleared to cross the border to come into the United States. Thanks to that policy, murders, robberies, gang violence, drug trafficking or smuggling, and human trafficking were all at a lower rate. The wall and control of the borders was on Trump's mind when he was running his campaign, which was the reason for the border's being well controlled immediately after he took office. Under Trump, Americans did not have to live in fear of anything, especially invasion of the border, as their lives and their privacy were protected. Citizens now have to hire private armed guards to protect their families because it looks and feels as if their country has failed to protect them from the migrant surge at the borders. Some of these migrants, when approached by border agents, try to run away and, in so doing, hit, kill, or run over security workers, sheriffs, and regular citizens. It may surprise you to learn that some of these individuals have crossed the border two or three times, even up to five times, because it is wide open. Some of the ones who run away from border patrol end up at citizens' front doors armed or with drugs, ready to fight their way in. Their numbers are in the millions now. Fentanyl and other drugs, even ones deadlier than fentanyl, come across our border now. The truth is that a well-controlled border should be able to prevent all the bad things and problems that come with uncontrolled borders.

Trump gave jobs to Americans, not to the cartels, who were smuggling illegal immigrants, delivering drugs, and making money in broad daylight safely, while good citizens and their food deliveries were in danger. Now people are packed into trucks inappropriately to cross the border. Some of the migrants are unable to shower or change their clothes. Some have died, and some are on suicide watch for cutting themselves because they were packed into overwhelmed shelters, which were unprepared for their coming. Border patrol agents are dying in high-speed migrant chases. Gas stations are hiring armed security guards to protect their customers. Such things would never happen on the watch of a president who knows the importance of a secure border like Trump.

Former president Trump signed an executive order to prevent illegal immigrants from being counted for the purpose of redrawing congressional district lines after the 2020 census. "There used to be a time when you could proudly declare, 'I am a citizen of the United States,' but now the Left is trying to erase the existence of this concept and conceal the number of illegal aliens in our country," he said during the signing of the apportionment memorandum on ensuring US citizens are properly represented in Congress. "I will not stand for the effort to erode or tamper with the rights of American citizens." Trump signed this memorandum on the census so that illegal immigrants would not be counted. Former president Trump wants Americans to be wealthy again, strong again, proud again, safe again, and great again, and therefore he signed a deal to limit the number of asylum seekers accepted from Guatemala, which was also signed by the Guatemalan administration. The former president emphasized that the agreement would end the crisis at the border caused by the thousands of people fleeing from violence and killing in El Salvador, Honduras, and Guatemala by allowing us to know who and what was coming into this country and when.

The president celebrated the eve of Fourth of July 2020 in South Dakota at Mount Rushmore National Memorial, where the faces of George Washington, Abraham Lincoln, Thomas Jefferson, and Theodore Roosevelt are carved. Since 2009, no fireworks had been displayed or enjoyed over Mount Rushmore, an important landmark in South Dakota, but that changed when Trump became president of the United States. On the eve of the 244th birthday of the United States, July 3, 2020, he signed an executive order to create the National Garden of American Heroes, an outdoor park to honor the greatest Americans, some of whom are as follows:

Benjamin Franklin, founding father of the United States, who was born on January 17, 1706, and who died on April 17, 1790, was an American polymath who was active as a writer, scientist, inventor, statesman, diplomat, printer, publisher, and political philosopher. Martin Luther King Jr. (January 15, 1929–April 4, 1968), an American Baptist minister and activist, was one of the most prominent leaders of the civil rights movement from 1955 until his assassination in 1968. Davy Crockett, former United States representative, who was born on August 17, 1786, and died on March 6, 1836, was an American folk hero, frontiersman, soldier, and politician. Often referred to in popular culture as "King of the Wild Frontier," Crockett represented Tennessee in the United States House of Representatives and served in the Texas revolution. Harriet Tubman, American abolitionist and social activist, died on March 10, 1913. After escaping enslavement, Tubman made some thirteen missions to rescue approximately seventy enslaved people, including her family and friends, using a network of antislavery activists and a safe house known as the Underground Railroad. Ronald Wilson Reagan, who was born on February 6, 1911, and died on June 5, 2004, was an American politician and actor who served as the fortieth president of the United States. He previously had served as the governor of California and as the president of the Screen Actors Guild. Jackie Robinson, who was born on January 31, 1919, and died on October 24, 1972, became the first African American to play Major League Baseball in the modern era. Robinson broke the baseball color line when he started at first base for the Brooklyn Dodgers on April 15, 1947. Amelia Earhart was an American aviation pioneer and writer. She was the first female aviator to fly solo across the Atlantic Ocean. Frederick Douglass, an American abolitionist, social reformer, orator, writer, and statesman, after escaping from slavery in Maryland, became a leader of the abolitionist movement in Massachusetts and New York, becoming famous for his oratory skills and intelligent antislavery writings.

For decades, Christians in Syria have been suffering and dying. Donald Trump knows well of the persecution they suffered. Feeling no sense of belonging, Christians were being punished with isolation, poor treatment, and even death. Trump gave Christians in Syria millions of dollars in aid to help with their situation and encouraged them not to abandon their faith. Former president Trump condemned the crucifixion of Christians and the brutal treatment of Christians, being the first president to call for an end to crucifixion of Christians at a United Nations meeting, the first president to step up for Christians and help them, demanding that all the maltreatment come to an end. During Trump's presidency, the United States imposed sanctions on Turkey after Turkey struck Kurdish people in Syria, including Christians. Trump raised tariffs on steel by 50 percent for Turkey, delayed negotiations on a billion-dollar trade deal with Turkey, imposed financial sanctions on Turkey, blocked Turkish ownership of US properties, and stopped Turkish officials from entering the United States because Turkish president Erdoğan abused Syria, obstructing the ceasefire and denying the Syrians human rights. Trump blocked Turkey from benefiting from the F-35 fighter jet after violating the rule against ordering military equipment from Russia.

Trump also signed a bill backing Hong Kong protesters and helping with their human rights, also saying that any Chinese who spied on the United States would be jailed or sent back home to China. He signed phase one of the China trade deal, which prohibits China from stealing US intellectual property, making knock-offs of US goods, and manipulating the currency and which includes China's commitment to double the purchases it makes from the United States, a provision worth billions of dollars, which was intended to continue to help US economic growth. This is the kind of move most of Trump's predecessors failed to make for the American people in terms of China and the extent of its influence. His delivery of jobs moved China to promise to invest billions of dollars into US products.

The United States Treasury Department imposed sanctions on two North Korean companies, North Korean Lodging Facility in China and Namgang Trading Corporation in Beijing, in October 2019, accusing them of illegally exporting workers in violation of United Nations sanctions. China was obligated to maintain its treaty with regard to Hong Kong but wanted to change from two autonomous communities to one country with one autonomy. Former president Trump intervened so that Hong Kong would maintain its autonomy because their freedoms were being degraded.

At home, Trump declared ten years' imprisonment for anyone who destroyed a monument or other government property. In August 2020, he gave one hundred thousand dollars of his salary (which was four hundred thousand dollars total) to be channeled into rebuilding those monuments. The rest of his salary went to other charities because, as was mentioned earlier, he refused to draw his salary as a president, saying that he would donate it to different charities such as those fighting the opioid crisis.

Trump signed the Great American Outdoors Act, a bill allocating money and resources to maintain national parks and US land; he devoted nearly three billion annually to conservation projects, which created many jobs.

Protecting the United States was one of his priorities. "Build a wall. If you build the wall, crime will fall," he said. Former president Trump built a wall at the southern US border, more than five hundred miles in length, which was not easy to accomplish politically, but he did it—and he did it to properly secure US territory and protect Americans from the danger and harm that comes along with the illegal crossing into this country of migrants, among whom sometimes are gang members and killers, literally pouring in, and some of whom kill innocent US citizens. Then there are the rapists, never mind the illegal drugs that are pouring in across the border, such as fentanyl and cocaine, along with other dangerous drugs and alcoholic beverages, all of which end up in the hands of our children, who become victims. The states on the border that are most concerning are Texas, Arizona, and New Mexico. Donald Trump simply would not put US citizens or the people of the world in harm's way, including border agents, children, and illegal immigrants. Our failure to finish building the wall has cost American lives, along with costing a fortune and costing us our future. He was a visionary who said that if the United States did not take care, then China would eat its lunch. Well, China is standing tall and is well able today, spying anyhow, both with balloons in the sky, passing over some of our military bases, and with cranes in the water—and maybe with other methods we know not of. With what is going on, it might not be only lunch but also breakfast and dinner because the Chinese are in their own country, in the sky, and also at our border.

Trump supported fracking, which led him to sign an order to stop people from banning fracking in the future. In Maine, he opened five thousand miles of ocean that had been closed by the previous administration, allowing fishermen to catch fish, lobsters, and crabs. He signed an order to prohibit the teaching of racism in the United States, but he promoted the 1776 Act to teach our children the glory of the United States. Former president Trump also signed an executive order banning the United States from investing in thirty-one Chinese companies that supported the Chinese military's owning of shares in the Chinese technology and telecommunications firm Tellright, the effective date being January 11, 2021. He was not afraid to label China as a currency manipulator; not since 1994 had any country been labeled as such by the United States.

I see former president Trump as the John the Baptist of our time. He is a great man, a prophet who prepares the way of the Lord. He makes the crooked places straight, and mends the bent places to be level, and announces the coming of the Messiah. I remember him preaching, telling Americans to repent and mend their ways, otherwise "China will eat your lunch." But the United States did not listen to him. Former president Trump indeed made the crooked places straight, but his successor canceled many of his policies, which still today continues to affect the United States poorly. The cancelations caused problems in areas such as the border, foreign policy, and national security. The wars that are happening now did not happen under Trump because of certain policies he put in place. Today it looks as if China has eaten all our aforementioned breakfasts, lunches, and dinners. You know this is true because of all China's manipulation of power, spying on the United States both from the land and up above in space, sizing the United States up in almost every area and also buying US land for its own purposes. China owns between three hundred thousand and four hundred thousand acres of land here in the United States, whether the land that came from buying companies or farmland.

How many acres of land does the United States own in China? And all the countries who are not supposed to talk down to the United States are now talking down to us. John the Baptist mended the way of the Lord and straightened up the crooked places, just as the wise former president Donald J. Trump has done. He has done it once for the American people, and he will do it again. He made the crooked places straight by making peace almost around the entire world. He caused Christians and Muslims of every denomination to live together in peace. He does not like war. There was no fighting during his time in office because he encouraged the world to live in peace. He straightened the crooked places by creating jobs. African Americans, Hispanic Americans, Asian Americans, and other people of color, men and women alike, were working, and the economy was good with no inflation. Trump supported agriculture in a big way, which people saw in their ability to buy enough food from the grocery stores to feed their families. When he was president, people were safe again out there in the world. He strongly supported Christianity. He has done it before and he will do it again, so that whoever will be president after him will stand on a good example of leadership.

Former president Trump granted clemency to a lot of people, including Roger Stone, a longtime friend of his and his campaign adviser, who was convicted on seven charges, including lying to Congress, and was sentenced to federal prison. Mr. Stone was quite honored, and he appreciated that President Trump used the great power granted to him by the Constitution to perform that act of kindness. Former junk bond king Michael Milken also had his sentence commuted. Trump commuted the sentence of former Illinois governor Rod Blagojevich, who served eight years of a fourteen-year prison sentence after he tried to sell the Senate seat that Barack Obama had left open once the latter decided to run for president. Other people whose sentences Trump commuted are Bernard Kerik, former commissioner of the New York City Police Department; Ariel Friedler; Paul Pogue; David Safavian; Angela Stanton;

Tynice Nichole Hall; Crystal Munoz; and Judith Negron. Trump pardoned former San Francisco Forty-Niners owner Edward DeBartolo Jr., who was convicted in a gambling fraud scandal. Trump also pardoned some turkeys; in November 2017, he pardoned Wishbone and Drumstick from Minnesota, the first turkeys to be named after their own body parts and the first to be pardoned by President Trump. US presidents have been pardoning turkeys prior to Thanksgiving for decades, as millions of turkeys are killed every November for Thanksgiving. In November 2018, Trump pardoned Peas and Carrots from South Dakota, and in November 2019, he pardoned Bread and Butter from North Carolina, letting them hang out in their room at the Willard Intercontinental Hotel in Washington before their pardoning day in November 2020. Trump continued to honor the White House tradition of officially pardoning the national Thanksgiving turkey. The candidates for 2020 were Corn and Cob from Iowa.

As president, Trump eliminated the individual

mandate penalty from Obamacare; gave us the cleanest water and cleanest air anywhere in the world; withdrew the United States from the Trans-Pacific Partnership job-killing regulations and the Paris Agreement; confronted China for its trade abuses, which affected our automobile manufacturers, and put in place reciprocal deals with China; and ended catch and release, meaning that migrants were no longer released into the United States of America after being captured by border control, which led to a decline in border apprehensions and the problems associated with unchecked immigration, including death, human trafficking, drug trafficking, gun smuggling, rape, and invasion of privacy.

In addition to signing phase one of the United States–China trade deal, Trump signed into law USMCA (the United States–Mexico–Canada Agreement) to end twenty-five years of US participation in the North American Free Trade Agreement (NAFTA), which is what had caused US manufacturing companies to move to other countries. Trump's trade agreement opened more doors and opportunities for trade, which gave a boost to farmers and to auto manufacturers and workers. Now American commodities could be exported the right way to other countries around the world, which helped to create the lowest unemployment rate in years and helped the economy. The China trade deal and the United States–Mexico–Canada trade deal are the two biggest trade deals of the century, and they were both made by Trump.

Trump is the first president to attend a March for Life, an annual pro-life march, the first sitting president to address an antiabortion gathering in person in the forty-seven years of the March for Life in Washington, DC, thereby giving dignity to life. The White House told the United Nations that there would be no international right to abortion under Trump. And the International Monetary Fund said that the low interest rates and reduced trade tensions would likely help world growth.

Also under Trump's administration, the United States vetoed the United Nations resolution calling for prosecution, rehabilitation, and reintegration of those participating in activities related to terrorism.

After a twenty-one-year-old student at Naval Air Station Pensacola student who was also a member of the Royal Saudi Air Force killed three of his colleagues, Trump took action immediately, calling for a new method of screening and vetting of Saudis and other foreign students. Trump does not sit things out or back away from taking action when the United States is hurt. With Trump's encouragement, Saudi Arabia ended an old gender segregation mandate that stipulated men and women use separate doors to enter places like restaurants and also pushed for social reform, including lifting of the ban against women in movie theaters. Now women in Saudi Arabia can go out and watch a movie, and social life has improved for Saudis in general. Women have been given privileges they were denied before; for example, women are now permitted to drive, play soccer/football, go to school, and own and run their own businesses.

Trump signed an order to remove protections from some waterways to aid developers in environmental rollback. And our forty-fifth president was the first to be named grand marshal of the Daytona 500 by NASCAR. He signed billions of dollars in defense bills to help the military, help the new space force, and protect US allies in space. Thousands of Americans joined the workforce with paid leave for federal workers.

Trump prohibited Title X taxpayer funding of the abortion industry, saying he did so "because Democrats wanted to rip babies from their mothers' womb[s] in the ninth month" per the Mexico City policy. The Mexico City policy, sometimes referred to by its critics as the global gag rule, is a former US government policy that blocked federal funding for any nongovernmental organizations that provided abortion counseling or referrals, recommended the decriminalization of abortion, or expanded abortion services. Trump also stopped federal funding of fetal tissue research. He always believed that every child, born and unborn alike, is made in the image of God and has a purpose in life.

Donald Trump was the first US president to attend the New York City Veterans Day Parade. Under his administration, our nation saw its lowest rate of veteran unemployment since 2000, a period of nearly twenty years. Trump established a twenty-four-hour hotline for veterans, increased veteran spending, increased military pay, and expanded the defense budget every year. He introduced the Office of Accountability through Veterans Affairs and expanded private health-care options. He made sure veterans of the wars in Vietnam and elsewhere in Asia were treated equally as other veterans. Some of these veterans were exposed to Agent Orange in combat depending on where they were located. Such people exposed to Agent Orange have an increased risk of contracting diseases such as diabetes, Parkinson's, and cancer. If you were exposed to Agent Orange during military service, you may qualify for VA disability benefits. The military sprayed Agent Orange and other tactical herbicides during the

Vietnam War. Former president Trump signed a bill to help any former service member who was exposed to Agent Orange. It took many years to get that done, but Trump is used to getting things done. He has a caring heart, quenching the Syrian crisis after thirty days instead of ten years. He put a stop to the Iraq War and the nineteen-year Afghanistan war, after trillions of dollars had been spent and millions of lives had been lost. From 2003, the start of the Iraq War, to the time Trump came into office, the number of Christians throughout the world had decreased from millions to thousands. He tried to make peace anywhere he could around the world. On the world stage, Trump called on the United Nations to help stop religious persecution of Christians.

Under Trump's management, more NATO allies started paying their fair share of dues, paying billions of dollars in 2016 and billions throughout the four years of his administration. Trump imposed a $2.4 billion tariff on French goods after the new French digital service tax, which unfairly discriminated against US technology companies. He was ready to sanction Turkey if they bought any Russian aircraft, missiles, or weapons. The sanctions he imposed on Iran prevented the Iranians from selling their crude oil abroad, which crushed their economy and, incidentally, prevented them from fighting Ukraine.

Lately, Beijing and Moscow have been threatening and sizing up the United States, and I have seen only one man stop them. That man is Trump. He does not like war, but he will sanction the hell out of any country that dares cross the line. He is capable. If the United States is a beautiful giant tree standing in front of you, then there must be a Trump leaf, if not a Trump root. Donald Trump is a visionary; that is why he said, "China will eat your lunch." He has already seen it, and he can fix all that is going wrong now, and fix it fast and well. Trump will not tolerate any country or anything else that is sizing up the United States and its interests. He signed an executive order closing down a certain app, saying that the Chinese were using it to spy on Americans and gain access to their personal information and discover where they were located. He placed tariffs on companies that left the United States of America to establish operations in other countries. He signed an order to pull the United States from an agreement to show preferential economic treatment to Hong Kong in trade, saying that Hong Kong did not merit such treatment because it was no longer autonomous. He signed this order after China put in place a new security law there. Hong Kong would be treated the same as mainland China, he said.

The Trump administration gave hope to the effort to preserve the Everglades. In 2020, he urged Congress to approve the sum of two hundred million dollars for an Everglades restoration project to take place over twenty years, and he upped the amount to two hundred fifty million dollars in the 2021 national budget. The restoration work included improvement of the water infrastructure. Committed to protecting the Everglades, one of Floridas' state treasures, Trump provided federal funds. Under his administration, New Jersey rebuilt the Portal Bridge over the Hackensack River with federal assistance, making the bridge higher so that when river traffic encounters the bridge, the bridge does not have to open and close to allow the traffic to pass beneath. Trump signed some million dollars in funding to fight reptiles that posed a danger in the coastal regions, especially Florida, and signed a bill allocating billions of dollars to renovate the airport in Panama, Florida. He signed into law pharmaceutical transparency for doctors and patients, and also a law reducing prescription drug costs. He renegotiated the South Korea trade deal. Thanks to his friendship with the world, he became the first United States president to cross the military demarcation line located in the demilitarized zone in North Korea, invited to do so by Chairman Kim Jong Un, who also let President Trump know that he was willing to close all North Korea's nuclear sites, remove them, and stop the testing of rockets and missiles. Trump signed a measure instituting a federal grant program to preserve Indigenous languages. He conducted air strikes against the Iranian-backed militia Hezbollah, which also targeted the United States, who were building places to house their troops and their Iraqi allies. That action prevented Iraq from doing more harm to our troops, with deportation, command, and control buses belonging to Hezbollah. A rocket attack also killed top Iranian military commander Qasem Soleimani, whom Trump called an enemy of the United States. He cotributed to so many death and disability of American troops, losing their hands, legs and body parts.

Trump signed for billions of dollars to be sent to Puerto Rico to rebuild its electric infrastructure and also rebuild schools three years after Hurricane Maria hit them hard. Trump wanted to stop the indoctrination intended by the 1619 Project and introduced the 1776 Commission, which he created to ensure that every American child learns that they live in the greatest nation in the world and, indeed, the best nation in the history of the world. He wants the United States to be the favorite nation, to pay the lowest price for medical care, to achieve price transparency in medicine, to achieve low prescription costs, and to ensure low health insurance premiums.

On September 2, 2020, Trump declared Wilmington, North Carolina, as the first World War II Heritage City. He was present that day at this battleground port city.

Former president Trump has a good signature and gives a good handshake. Always, I see his domination whenever he gives anybody, including any president, a handshake. It is inborn for him. He is fearless when it comes to the United States getting its fair share, protecting its own interests, and being right on the world stage or anywhere on earth. Mr. President, I want you to know that politics is a dangerous and dirty game, but the United States loves you. Continue to do anything you can for the United States. God bless the United States.

Behind every successful man is a great woman, and so behind every successful president is a great first lady. Hello to former first lady Melania Trump, a tall, beautiful, humble woman, a model with the hair of an angel and long legs—a naturally beautiful woman. She is tall, tough, thoughtful, family-oriented, and very stylish, her wardrobe always being modern and pretty because she is the greatest model God ever created. In my point of view, elegance is her legacy. The way she stands, carries herself, walks, looks, talks, and handles anything at all exudes elegance. In addition to being a former model, Melania Trump has launched jewelry and skin-care lines. She is bilingual and is the second first lady to be born outside the United States.

Melania is the devoted mother of Barron William Trump. Because she is tough and thoughtful, it was possible for her to manage mothering a child while on the campaign trail, including being hands-on with her son's schoolwork and homework, and also teaching him to be respectful and responsible and to be a gentleman during their time in the White House.

Melania Trump is a role model for a lot of

women. She is beautiful inside and outside, which is how she is able to hold the Trump family, which is a big family, together and keep everyone happy and connected with love for one another. Hopefully the Trumps forget about politics sometimes. It is good to give credit to the one who deserves credit, so I give credit to Melania Trump. It is a big and an important job to keep a family together, never mind one with different mothers.

Melania Trump's sense of style was evident in her decorating of the Christmas trees all in red her first year at the White House. A lot of people saw these decorations in person, whereas many others saw them on television all around the world, which made many people want to visit the White House to see the decorations firsthand.

An amazing mother and an incredible, virtuous woman, Melania Trump visited some African countries, for example, Ghana, Kenya, Malawi, and Egypt, also visiting their schools, their hospitals, and their families and encouraging the youth to dream big, to think bigger, and to be the best. She believes in leaving things better than one finds them. She called on lawmakers to pass a law that would allow anyone struggling with opioid addiction to seek help without shame, also championing the cause of finding a cure for opioid addiction and neonatal crisis treatment and management. The former first lady entered the national dialogue, meeting with women both here at home and abroad. She loves American children and cares for their well-being.

The former first lady met with governors' spouses for the betterment of our country. She encouraged protesters to protest in peace and with protection, and she told the family of George Floyd, an African American man murdered by a white Minneapolis police officer, to take heart. Because she is a beautiful model, different types of colorful flowers were used as decoration whenever she alone, or she and her husband together, traveled abroad. My favorite was India, where the former first lady Melania Trump and the former president Donald Trump played by making a bed of flowers with different bright colors. While in India, the former first lady visited the Delhi Government School and attended what they called a happiness class, a program developed by the Indian government for children in nursery school to grade eight. In happiness class, there are no textbooks and no exams. During the daily thirty-to-thirty-five-minute lesson, teachers lead the students in meditation, creative exercises, storytelling, and activities focused on students' emotional and mental health. Melania Trump gave all the students a hug after the class.

The former first lady constructed a tennis court at the White House. Also, she recognized that the Rose Garden hadn't been changed since 1962 and needed to be elevated, renovations that now accommodate both able-bodied and disabled people. She redesigned the Rose Garden to better resemble its 1962 layout, which was its state during the Kennedy administration—which, by the way, Melania Trump likes Jackie Kennedy. One of the main reasons for the renovations was to make the place accessible to citizens with a disability, adding audiovisual support for broadcasting purposes and to make the setting more enjoyable for all people. Melania Trump emphasized that planting a garden involves hard work, but she was determined to do it for a brighter future, beautifying the Rose Garden and preserving it for future generations. Melania Trump thanked the people who helped to redo the iconic and truly gorgeous space to better match its original design. The former first lady delivered her 2020 Republican National Convention speech from the Rose Garden, which is famous for its closeness and accessibility to the Oval Office.

The former president and former first lady worked very hard for the American people, delivering on all their campaign promises and doing much more. Every American, whether white, of African descent, Latino, or Asian, was impacted positively under the Trump administration. It is tradition that the first lady of the United States use the platform of the highest office in the nation to advocate for a good cause during her tenure in the White House. Melania Trump used her good office to introduce the

Be Best initiative, the three pillars of which are the dangers of drug abuse, the importance of online safety, and the importance of children's well-being so they can fight bullying. Beautiful Melania Trump delivered for children and their well-being with the Be Best initiative, lamenting that it is rough for teenagers in this country and around the world. She said, "It is not good when our girls and boys are mocked or bullied as an example to the world. It has to start at home, calling upon adults to be role models for our younger ones, not hiding behind the internet." Proverbs 22:6 says, "Train up a child in the way he should go and when he is old, he will not depart from it, as well over this Jesus shall not depart from your mouth" (ESV). Joshua 1:8 reads, "Keep this book of the law always on your lips, meditate on it day and night so that you may be careful to do everything written in it, then you will be prosperous and successful." Melania Trump encouraged children to eat healthy fruits and vegetables.

The former first lady was tough on immigration,

even when the zero tolerance policy affected immigrant children who were separated from their families. As I write in 2023, the United States has had two first ladies who were immigrants, not born in the United States of America. First was Louisa Catherine Adams, wife of the sixth president of United States, John Quincy Adams. Louise Adams was an immigrant from London, England. The second first lady who is an immigrant is Melania Trump, wife of the forty-fifth president of the United States of America, Donald John Trump. Melania immigrated to the United States from the former Yugoslavia, which is now part of Novo Mesto, Slovenia. During the time the immigration policy that separated children from their families was in effect, our first lady swung into action right away because she is a champion for the welfare of our children. Also as a mother and an immigrant, she was just the first lady to settle the matter. The separations were hard for her to watch. Immediately she called our president's—her husband's—attention to it and advised him that people should be vetted before coming into our country. Under zero tolerance, the separation of children from their parents did not look good at all. It was one of the rare times when our president changed his mind on an issue, putting a stop to the separation because of our first lady's concern about children. Melania Trump is an immigrant herself, so she convinced her husband, the president of the United States of America, to cease the separation of families at the border. She met with the border agents and asked them how she could help and also visited the children and encouraged them, telling them that the matter would go before the courts and that they would be reunited with their families as soon as possible.

Hello to Honorable Jim Jordan, member of the Republican Party, chairman of the House Judiciary Committee and representative of the Fourth Congressional District of Ohio. Jim Jordan is a staunch Republican, a Christian, a Trumper, and a conservative. He was awarded the Presidential Medal of Freedom by former president Trump. Jordan is ever ready to tackle matters on the House floor. He fights for and defends Republicans. A friend in need is a friend indeed. Jim Jordan is not only a Republican but also a friend of Republicans.

Hello to a man who endorsed my president, the forty-fifth, possibly forty-seventh president of the United States. He has many assets, but for the sake of peace, love, and inclusivity, and also to prevent online censorship in the country, he bought Twitter for billions of dollars and renamed it X. The brain behind SpaceX and Tesla Motors, who is a loyal citizen of the United States of America, Elon Reeve Musk.

The condition of my country, which I love very much, is what pushed me to write *A Good Signature*. The country is deteriorating with insecurity, inflation, a bad economy, smash-and-grab, insufficient oil and gas, a wide-open border that has resulted in the worst and most dangerous wave of migration ever into the United States with immigrants from different parts of the world, from countries that are either our allies or our adversaries, and weakness to the extreme.

Almost every country is sizing up the United States. The United States has lost its greatness and has lost respect, with Americans being easily killed around the world without the perpetrators fearing any consequences from the United States. There once was a time when anywhere in the world, you would not go free if you killed an American. But now the US flag is burned abroad and also here at home by protesters.

God's own country is what we want. Trump restored the United States to greatness during the four years he was in office. Seeing is believing. He has done it before, and he will do it again, this next time exceeding expectations. Once an economy builder, always be an economy builder. Trump is an economy grower.

Printed in the United States
by Baker & Taylor Publisher Services